Praise for *He's Just Not That Into You*

"Finally, honest answers to our guy woes."   —*Seventeen*

"Evil genius."   —*New York Times*

"Ruthless romance advice."   —*Us Weekly*

"Brims with straight talk about the boy-meets-girl game, delivered with hefty doses of humor from the Y chromosome's mouth."   —*USA Today*

"No ego-soothing platitudes. No pop psychology. No cute relationship tricks. *He's just not that into you.*"
                                    —*Washington Post*

"Self-help titles don't come much more chilling than this."
                                            —*People*

"This book could save a generation of women who would be wasting their lives waiting by the phone."   —*Boston Herald*

"A surprisingly fascinating addition to the cultural canon of single, urban life."   —*Los Angeles Times*

"No psycho mumbo-jumbo here. The bestseller that has women talking—and laughing out loud . . . is a refreshing look at how men really feel about women."   —*Seattle Times*

"Smart, funny and surprisingly upbeat."   —*Publishers Weekly*

he's just
not that
into you

The No-Excuses Truth to Understanding Guys

The Newly Expanded Edition

greg behrendt
and
liz tuccillo

 SIMON SPOTLIGHT ENTERTAINMENT
New York London Toronto Sydney

SIMON SPOTLIGHT ENTERTAINMENT

An imprint of Simon & Schuster

1230 Avenue of the Americas, New York, New York 10020

Copyright © 2004, 2006 by Greg Behrendt and Liz Tuccillo

All rights reserved, including the right of reproduction in whole or in part in any form.

SIMON SPOTLIGHT ENTERTAINMENT and related logo are trademarks of
Simon & Schuster, Inc.

Manufactured in the United States of America

10 9 8 7 6 5 4 3 2

Library of Congress Cataloging-in-Publication Data

Behrendt, Greg.

He's just not that into you : the no-excuses truth to understanding guys /
by Greg Behrendt and Liz Tuccillo.—1st ed.

p. cm.

ISBN-13: 978-0-689-87474-1 (original hc)

ISBN-10: 0-689-87474-X (original hc)

1. Man-woman relationships. 2. Men—Psychology. 3. Men—Attitudes.
4. Rejection (Psychology). 5. Communication—Sex differences.
I. Tuccillo, Liz. II. Title.

HQ801.B37 2004

306.7—dc22

2004011658

ISBN-13: 978-1-4169-4740-0 (expanded hc edition)

ISBN-10: 1-4169-4740-X (expanded hc edition)

This book is dedicated to all the lovely ladies out there
whose stories inspired us to write this book.
May we never need to write another one.

note to the reader

The stories you will read in this book are illustrative examples, not based on specific events or people. No matter what anyone might think, they are not transparent attempts to publicly mock our friends, enemies, or exes.

(However, we're not going to say the thought didn't cross our minds.)

—Greg and Liz

acknowledgments

There are a few people whom without their involvement this book would never have come to be. First and foremost, we must thank all the supremely talented inhabitants of the writers' room of *Sex and the City*. They are: Cindy Chupack, Jenny Bicks, Amy B. Harris, Julia Sweeney, Julie Rottenberg, Elisa Zuritsky (who together wrote the amazing episode that first brought the "He's just not that into you" message to the world), and of course, our brilliant leader, Michael Patrick King. Much love and deepest gratitude go to all of them for their support, generosity, and superhuman funniness.

We would like to thank all those who facilitated this crazy book idea right from the start. They are John Melfi, Sarah Condon, Richard Oren, and everyone else who pitched in to help at HBO. Super agent and friend Greg Cavic at ICM got the whole ball rolling, and big thanks to Julie James for moving it all along when necessary. Our deepest gratitude goes to our book agent, Andy Barzvi, who was the first person to take this book to heart, and then managed to sell the hell out of it. Many thanks to our editor, Patrick Price, who has never been anything less than a gentleman and a scholar.

Thank you to the men and women who filled out our questionnaires, told us stories, asked us questions, and kept us honest. We thank all our friends and families for their enthusiastic encouragement, particularly Shirley Tuccillo and Kristen Behrendt.

Last but not least, we must thank Amiira Ruotola Behrendt, whose collaboration, passion, humor, talent, love, and extraordinarily foxy great example made this book rock.

table of contents

foreword

The publishers of *He's Just Not That Into You* asked us if we wanted to write another chapter or add anything to the book for future editions. My response was, "Are you kidding me? It's perfect." But then I reconsidered my position. Do I have more to say on the subject? Not really. I feel we pretty much covered it. But the point of view I *hadn't* considered was what it's like to be a woman living in the post–*He's Just Not That Into You* world.

Hmmm . . . I pondered who could possibly have thoughts on this subject. I couldn't think of anyone, so I took a nap. Then Liz called. Surprisingly, as a single woman living in New York City, she felt she had some information she wanted to share. Thus was born the first of the two bonus chapters at the end of this edition.

Also, since the publication of *He's Just Not That Into You* I've been asked a million questions. Everything from "Did you think the book would be such a success?" to "Who the fuck do you think you are?" (The latter from a fairly upset marine who maybe wasn't as into his lady as he should have been. Sorry, man.)

As to the first question, the answer is a resounding no! It's not that I didn't think it was a good idea; it's that I didn't have any idea there would be such a need. My goal was just to write a book so that I could tell my friends, "Hey, I wrote that pink-and-green relationship book at Urban Outfitters." Just kidding! You have to understand that both Liz and my wife, Amiira, had to convince me that such a book should be written. It's not like I woke up one day and said, "I need to wake women up to what's going on in their relationships, and then I'm going to the gym." I really had no idea that women were spending so much time obsessing over men. And I don't mean that in a negative way—I just didn't know. And I was sort of dumbstruck that a book like this hadn't been written before. That's why Amiira and Liz were so emphatic that I do it, because they knew a book like this did not exist.

But after our appearance on *The Oprah Winfrey Show*, Liz and I suddenly became "relationship experts," which is hilarious to me, because if you ever dated me you would not believe me to be an expert on anything. We were asked to comment on all things dating, from celebrity dating to the mating rituals of dogs (they are quite similar, actually). Needless to say, I was overwhelmed by the response to the book. My website crashed three times due to the amount of traffic—mostly by women with questions they didn't feel were addressed in the book, though I tended to disagree. (Maybe we didn't use his name, but he's in there!) Sometimes I would write back things like "Hey, you've just written a ten-page e-mail about your relationship to a comedian. How do *you* think it's going?" But then I would give my assessment. I also got quite a few e-mails from men, and not just the "If I ever see you in a dark alley, you are going down like a sack of lead potatoes" kind, but the "I like this girl but she never returns my calls" kind.

There were some questions that kept coming up *over and over again*—some from people who had loved the book, and some from people who were really not members of the Liz and Greg fan club. The truth is, I loved the questions. We loved it. One person asked if it bothers me that people now come up to me in public and ask me questions about their relationships. And the answer is "Never!" Not even the time I stood shirtless in the dressing room of a fancy department store and explained to the pretty salesgirl that if he doesn't want to marry her because she doesn't speak German, then he's just not . . . well, you know the rest.

I hope this book will answer some questions for you, and I hope your current and future relationships will be the better because of it. That's why we wrote it—because we're totally into you.

—Greg

Introduction by Liz

It started out just like any other day. We were all working in the writers' room of *Sex and the City*, talking, pitching ideas, our personal love lives weaving in and out of the fictional lives we were creating in the room. And just like on any other day, one of the women on staff asked for feedback on the behavior of a man whom she liked. He was giving her mixed messages—she was confused. We were happy to pitch in and pick apart all the signs and signals of his actions. And just like on any other day, after much analysis and debate, we concluded that she was *fabulous,* he must be scared, he's never met a woman as great as her, he is intimidated, and she should just give him time. But on this day, we had a male consultant in the room—someone who comes in a couple of times a week to give feedback on story lines and gives a great straight-male perspective: Greg Behrendt. On this day, Greg listened intently to the story and our reactions, and then said to the woman in question, "Listen, it sounds like he's just not that into you."

We were shocked, appalled, amused, horrified, and above all, intrigued. We sensed immediately that this man might be speaking the truth. A truth that we, in our combined hundred years of dating experience, had never considered, and definitely never considered saying out loud. "Okay, he might have a point," we reluctantly agreed. "But Greg couldn't possibly understand *my* very busy and complicated possible future husband." Soon we went around the room, Greg, the all-knowing Buddha, listening to story after mixed-message story. We had excuses for all these men, from broken dialing fingers to difficult childhoods. In the end, one by one, they were shot down by Greg's powerful silver bullet. Greg made us see, after an enormous amount of effort, that if a (sane) guy really likes you, there ain't nothing that's going to get in his way. And if he's not sane, why would you want him? He could back it up too: He had years of playing the field, being the bad boy, being the good boy, and then finally falling in love and marrying a really fantastic woman.

A collective epiphany burst forth in the room, and for me in particular. All these years I'd been complaining about men and their mixed messages; now I saw they weren't mixed messages at all. I was the one that was mixed up. Because the fact was, these men had simply not been that into me.

Now, at first glance it seems that this should have been demoralizing to us, it should have sent us all into a tailspin. Yet the opposite was true. Knowledge is power, and more importantly, knowledge saves us time. I realized that from that day forward I would be spared hours and hours of waiting by the phone, hours and hours of obsessing with my girlfriends, hours and hours of just hoping his mixed messages really meant "I'm in love with you and want to be with you." Greg reminded us that we were all beautiful, smart, funny women, and we shouldn't be wasting our time figuring out why a guy isn't calling us. As Greg put it, we shouldn't waste the pretty.

It's hard. We're taught that in life, we should try to look on the bright side, to be optimistic. Not in this case. In this case, look on the dark side. Assume rejection first. Assume you're the rule, not the exception. It's intoxicatingly liberating. But we also know it's not an easy concept. Because this is what we do: We go out with someone, we get excited about them, and then they do something that mildly disappoints us. Then they keep doing a lot more things that disappoint us. Then we go into hyper-excuse mode for weeks or possibly months, because the last thing we want to think is that this great man that we are so excited about is in the process of turning into a creep. We try to come up with some explanation for why they're behaving that way, any explanation, no matter how ridiculous, than the one explanation that's the truth: He's just not that into me.

That's why we've included questions from women taken from real situations. They represent the basic excuses we all use that keep us in situations far longer than we should be. So read, enjoy, and hopefully learn from other women's confusion. And above all, if the guy you're dating doesn't seem to be completely into you, or you feel the need to start "figuring him out," please consider the glorious thought that he might just not be that into you. And then free yourself to go find the one that is.

Introduction by Greg

So I'm sitting in the writers' room at *Sex and the City* pondering my good fortune to be the only straight male on the predominantly female writing staff (actually I'm just eating a cookie), when the writers begin talking about guys they're seeing. This is a common occurrence, as it is part of the writing process for a show that explores romantic relationships. It is endlessly fascinating. I know that sounds sarcastic, but I'm being for real.

So on this particular day, one of the ladies pipes up with, "Greg, you're a guy." She is very observant, this one, for I am indeed a guy. Then she says, "So I've been seeing this guy. . . . Well, I think I have." I know the answer. "See, we went to a movie and it was great. I mean he didn't hold my hand, but that's cool. I don't like to hold hands." Still know the answer. "But afterward he kissed me in the parking lot. So I asked if he wanted to come over, but he had a really important meeting in the morning so he didn't come over." C'mon. Are you kidding me? Know it!

So I ask, "Have you heard from him?"

"Well, that's the thing. This was like a week ago"—now *you* should know the answer—"and then today he e-mails me and is like, 'Why haven't I heard from you?'"

I stare at her for a moment while the answer is bursting

out of my eyeballs. (Oh, ladies, you make me so mad sometimes!) Here is this beautiful, talented, super-smart girl, who is a writer on an award-winning TV show, a show known for its incisive observations about men, who you would think could have her pick of just about any dude around. This superstar of a woman is confused about a situation that to me is so clear. Actually, confused is the wrong word, because she's too smart for that. She's hopeful, not confused. But the situation is hopeless, so I break the news to her: "He's just not that into you."

And let me tell you, that's the good news, because wasting time with the wrong person is just time wasted. And when you do move on and find your right person, believe me, you're not going to wish you had gotten to spend more time with Stinky the Time-Waster or Freddy Can't-Remember-to-Call.

Look, I am not a doctor, neither real nor imagined. But I am an expert that should be listened to because of one very important thing: I'm a guy—a guy that has had his fair share of relationships and is willing to come clean about his behavior in them. Because I'm a guy, I know how a guy thinks, feels, and acts, and it's my responsibility to tell you who we really are. I'm tired of seeing great women in bullshit relationships.

When a guy is into you, he lets you know it. He calls, he shows up, he wants to meet your friends, he can't keep his eyes or hands off of you, and when it's time to have sex, he's more than overjoyed to oblige. I don't care if he's starting his new job as the president of the United States the next morning at 0400 (that's 4 A.M., ladies!). He's coming up!

Men are not complicated, although we'd like you to think

we are, as in "Things are really crazy right now. I've just got a ton of shit going on." We are driven by sex, although we'd like to pretend otherwise: "What? No, I was totally listening." And sadly (and most embarrassingly), we would rather lose an arm out a city bus window than tell you simply, "You're not the one." We are quite sure you will kill us or yourself or both—or even worse, cry and yell at us. We are pathetic. But the fact remains, even though we may not be saying it, we are *absolutely* showing it all the time. If a dude isn't calling you when he says he will, or making sure you know that he's dating you, then you already have your answer. Stop making excuses for him; his actions are screaming the truth: He's just not that into you.

Move on, sister! Cut your losses and don't waste your time. Why stay in some weird dating limbo when you can move on to what will surely be better territory? Don't want to hear it? Fine. Here's the answer you're looking for: "Hang in there, baby. He's not the loser everybody's telling you he is. If you wait and keep your mouth shut and call at exactly the right time and anticipate his moods and have no expectations about communication or your own sexual needs, you can have him!" But please don't be surprised when he dumps you or continues to drag you through a completely unsatisfying relationship.

We've heard it and you're sick of it. That's probably why you're in possession of this book now. You know you deserve to have a great relationship. We agree. So grab a highlighter and get started. Liz told you I was going to say it: Don't waste the pretty!

You Are All Dating the Same Guy

Hey. I know that guy you're dating.

Yeah, I do. He's that guy that's so tired from work, so stressed about the project he's working on. He's just been through an awful breakup and it's really hitting him hard. His parents' divorce has scarred him and he has trust issues. Right now he has to focus on his career. He can't get involved with anyone until he knows what his life is about. He just got a new apartment and the move is a bitch. As soon as it all calms down he'll leave his wife, girlfriend, crappy job. God, he's so complicated.

He is a man made up entirely of your excuses. And the minute you stop making excuses for him, he will completely disappear from your life. Are there men who are too busy or have been through something so horrible that makes it hard for them to get involved? Yes, but there are so few of them that they should be considered urban legends. For as already suggested, a man would rather be trampled by elephants that are on fire than tell you that he's just not that into you. That's why we've written this book. We wanted to get the excuses out of the closet, so to speak, so they can be seen for exactly what they are: really bad excuses.

Hey—do you remember that movie when the girl waited around for the guy to ask her out, then made excuses when he didn't? Then she slept with him when they were both drunk, and basically just hung around until they were kind of dating? Then he cheated on her, but because she knew deep down inside that if she forgave him and kept her expectations low and was really agreeable, she'd get him in the end? He was drunk at the wedding, but they lived miserably ever after in an unsatisfying relationship that was built on a shitty foundation? You don't? That's because those movies don't get made, because that's not what love is like. People are inspired to do remarkable things to find and be with the one they love. Big movies are made about it, and every relationship you admire bursts with a greatness that you hope for in your own life. And the more you value yourself, the more chance you'll have of getting it. So read these excuses, have a laugh, and then . . . put them all to rest. You're worth it.

he's just not that into you if he's not asking you out

*Because if he likes you,
trust me, he will ask you out*

Many women have said to me, "Greg, men run the world." Wow. That makes us sound pretty capable. So tell me, why would you think we could be incapable of something as simple as picking up the phone and asking you out? You seem to think at times that we're "too shy" or we "just got out of something." Let me remind you: Men find it very satisfying to get what they want. (Particularly after a difficult day of running the world.) If we want you, we will find you. If you don't think you gave him enough time to notice you, take the time it took you to notice him and divide it by half.

Now you begin the life-changing experience of reading our book. We have put the stories we have heard and questions we've been asked in a simple question-and-answer format. If you're lucky, you'll read the following questions and know what they are: Excuses that women have made for their unsatisfying situations. If you're not so lucky, we've also included handy titles to clue you in.

The "Maybe He Doesn't Want to Ruin the Friendship" Excuse

Dear Greg,

I'm so disappointed. I have this friend that I've known platonically for about ten years. He lives in a different city and recently he was in town for work, so we met for dinner. All of a sudden it felt like we were on a date. He was completely flirting with me. He even said to me, as he was checking me out, "So, what, you're working the whole 'model thing' now?" (That's flirting, right?) We both agreed that we should get together again soon. Well, Greg, I'm disappointed because it's been two weeks and he hasn't called me. Can I call him? He might be nervous about turning the friendship into romance. Can't I give him a nudge now? Isn't that what friends are for?

Jodi

FROM THE DESK OF GREG

Dear Friendly Girl,

Two weeks is two weeks, except when it's ten years and two weeks. That's how long ago he decided whether or not he

10

could date a model or a girl who looks like one. Can you be a pal and give him a nudge? Nudge away, friendster—but watch how fast that nudge doesn't get a return phone call. And if your dinner/date did feel different to him, it's been two weeks and he's had time to think about it and decide he's just not that into you. Here's the truth: Guys don't mind messing up a friendship if it could lead to sex, whether it be a "fuck buddy" situation or a meaningful romance. Go find someone that lives in your zip code who will be rocked to the core by your deep conversation and model looks.

I hate to tell you, but that whole "I don't want to ruin the friendship" excuse is a racket. It works so well because it seems so wise. Sex *could* mess up a friendship. Unfortunately, in the entire history of mankind, that excuse has never ever been used by someone who actually means it. If we're really excited about someone, we can't stop ourselves—we want more. If we're friends with someone and attracted to them, we're going to want to take it further. And please, don't tell me he's just "scared." The only thing he's scared of—and I say this with *a lot* of love—is how not attracted to you he is.

The "Maybe He's Intimidated by Me" Excuse

Dear Greg,
   I have a crush on my gardener. He's been potting the plants on my patio. It was hot, I saw him without his shirt on, he was hot, and now I'm hot for him. I brought out some beers and we talked. I think he wants

to ask me out but is afraid, because he is my hired man. In this situation, can't I ask him out?

Cherie

FROM THE DESK OF GREG

Dear My Secret Garden,

He's capable of asking you out. Haven't you ever seen a porno? Hope he gets there before the pizza guy. But seriously, if he didn't pick up the vibe after the beer garden, it has nothing to do with you being his big boss lady. Time to stop and smell the bad news: He's just not that into you.

Let me say it again, sexual harassment rules and workplace memos notwithstanding, a guy will ask out a woman of higher status if he's into her. He might need a little more encouragement than normal, I'll give you that. You might have to lead Johnny the Office Boy or Philippe the Exterminator to water, but you better not help him ask you out. Once again, ladies, a wink and a smile will do it.

By the way, why are you dating the exterminator?

Just kidding, he's a good guy.

The "Maybe He Wants to Take It Slow" Excuse

Dear Greg,

There's this guy who calls me all the time. He's recently divorced, and in AA. We got back in touch recently, had lots of phone calls, and then hung out twice in one week and it was real cool. No flirting or making out or anything, but fun. Since then, he calls me all the time but doesn't ever suggest we see each other in person again. It's like he got scared or something. I would understand if because of the divorce/alcoholic/starting-a-whole-new-life stuff he wanted to take things slow. But he still calls me all the time to have long heart-to-heart talks. What the hell should I do with this guy?

Jen

FROM THE DESK OF GREG

Dear Pillow Talk,

Sadly, not wanting to see you in person is massive as far as dating obstacles go. And as far as the recently divorced/newly sober/starting-a-new-life parts, blah blah blah, I'm getting sleepy, it's hot, I'm going down for a nap. When I wake up from that nap I'll probably thrill to the news that your friend is taking control of his life. You, however, will still not be going on a date, because despite all your excuses for him, he's still not asking you out. Now, if you're a person who enjoys a slightly satisfying phone relationship, talk on! But at this point it seems like he's just not that into you. Be his friend if you're at all interested on that level, but move your romantic inclinations onto a more suitable future husband.

If a guy truly likes you, but for personal reasons he needs to take things slow, *he will let you know that immediately*. He won't keep you guessing, because he'll want to make sure you don't get frustrated and go away.

The "But He Gave Me His Number" Excuse

Dear Greg,

I met a really cute guy at a bar this week. He gave me his number and told me to give him a call sometime. I thought that was kind of cool, that he gave me control of the situation like that. I can call him, right?

Lauren

FROM THE DESK OF GREG

Dear Control Freak,

Did he give you control, or did he just get you to do the heavy lifting? What he just did was a magic trick: It *seems* like he gave you control, but really he now gets to decide if *he* wants to go out with *you*—or even return your call. Why don't you take Copperfield's number, roll it in a newspaper, pour milk in it, and make it disappear.

"Give me a call." "E-mail me." "Tell Joey we should all hang out sometime." *Don't let him trick you into asking him out.* When men want you, they do the work. I know it sounds old school, but when men like women, they ask them out.

The "Maybe He Forgot to Remember Me" Excuse

Dear Greg,

Okay, Greg. Listen to this one: I was at a conference for work and met a guy from another branch of my company. We hit it off immediately. He was just about to ask for my number, I swear, when the Big Blackout of 2003 happened. In the mayhem, I didn't get to give him my number. I think the Big Blackout of 2003 is a good enough excuse to call him, don't you think? It's only common courtesy for me to check up on him, right? If I don't call, he's probably going to be all sad thinking that *I'm* just not that into him.

Judy

FROM THE DESK OF GREG

Dear Judy Blackout,

The city blacked out. He didn't. You said you work for different branches of the same company. Certainly he wouldn't have to break a sweat to scroll through the company staff roster or interoffice e-mail listing to find you. And should he not be as resourceful as you are . . . I imagine that he has a mother, sister, or female friend that could show him how, if he was really interested.

P.S.: Shame on you for using an eastern seaboard disaster as an excuse to call a guy up.

Have faith. You made an impression. Leave it at that. If he likes you, he'll still remember you after the tsunami, flood, or Red Sox loss. If he doesn't, he's not worth your time. Know why? You are great. (Now, don't get cocky.)

The "Maybe I Don't Want to Play Games" Excuse

Dear Greg,

This is dumb. I know you're not supposed to call guys, but I call guys all the time because I don't care! I don't want to play games. I do whatever I want! I've called guys tons of times. You're such a square, Greg. Why do you think we can't call guys and ask them out?

Nikki

FROM THE DESK OF GREG

Dear Nikki,

Because we don't like it. Okay, some guys might like it, but they're just lazy. And who wants to go out with Lazy Guy? It's that simple. I didn't make the rules and I might not even agree with them. Please don't be mad at me, Nikki. I'm not advocating that women go back to the Stone Age. I just think you might want to be realistic in how capable you are of changing the primordial impulses that drive all of human nature.

Or maybe you're the chosen one.

Men, for the most part, like to pursue women. We like not knowing if we can catch you. We feel rewarded when we do.

Especially when the chase is a long one. We know there was a sexual revolution. (We loved it.) We know women are capable of running governments, heading multinational corporations, and raising loving children—sometimes all at the same time. That, however, doesn't make *men* different.

IT'S SO SIMPLE

Imagine right now that I'm leaping up and down and shaking my fist at the sky. I'm on my knees pleading with you. I'm saying this in a loud voice: "Please, if you can trust one thing I say in this book, let it be this: *When it comes to men, deal with us as we are, not how you'd like us to be.*" I know it's an infuriating concept—that men like to chase and you have to let us chase you. I know. It's insulting. It's frustrating. It's unfortunately the truth. My belief is that if you have to be the aggressor, if you have to pursue, if you have to do the asking out, nine times out of ten, he's just not that into you. (And we want you to believe you're one of the nine, ladies!) I can't say it loud enough: You, the superfox reading this book, are worth asking out.

HERE'S WHY THIS ONE IS HARD, by Liz

Well, it's obvious. Are you telling us that we have to just sit around and wait? I don't know about you, but I find that infuriating. I was brought up to believe that hard work and good planning are the keys to making your dreams come true. I spent my life making things happen for myself. I worked hard for my career, and was quite aggressive about it. I called people, made appointments, asked for favors. I took action. But now Greg is telling us that in this situation, we are supposed to do absolutely nothing. The guys get to pick. We're just supposed to put on our little dresses and do our hair and bat our eyes and hope *they* choose *us*. Why don't you just tie my corset too tight so I can faint in front of some man who'll scoop me out of the way just before the horse-drawn carriage runs over me? That'll get his attention.

Really, in this day and age, the hardest thing to do for many women, particularly me, is nothing. We like to scheme, make phone calls, have a plan. And I'm talking about more than just making sure our hair doesn't frizz. Most women who date, I would guess, don't have men throwing themselves at them every night of the week. Sometimes there's a long stretch during which nobody's asking us out. So when we see a guy that we feel might be a romantic possibility, it's even harder for us to take a backseat. That opportunity might not come back again for a long time.

But guess what: My way? Has sucked. Hasn't worked at all. I've never had a successful relationship with a guy that I've pursued. I'm sure there are many stories out there to the contrary. But for me, those guys end up getting back together with their ex-girlfriend, needing to take some time for themselves, or going out of town for business. Usually it doesn't even get that far. They usually just don't ever return my phone call. And let me tell you, that didn't make me feel very in control of anything.

Since I've been implementing Greg's handy-dandy "he's just not that into you" philosophy, I've been feeling surprisingly *more* powerful. Because if the men are asking you out, if the men have to get your attention, then you, in fact, are the one in control. There's no scheming and plotting. And there is something great about knowing that my only job is to be as happy as I can be about my life, and feel as good as I can about myself, and to lead as full and eventful a life as I can, so that it doesn't ever feel like I'm just waiting around for some guy to ask me out. And most importantly, it's good for us all to remember that we don't need to scheme and plot and beg to get someone to ask us out. We're fantastic.

THIS IS WHAT IT SHOULD LOOK LIKE, by Greg

One night I was drinking in a bar and flirting with the bartender. I asked for her number. She said, "I don't give out my phone number because guys rarely call me when they say they're going to. My name is Lindsey Adams, and if you want to call me, find my phone number." Which I did—the very next day. Do you know how many Lindsey Adamses there are in the phone book of a major city? Let's just say I talked to about eight or nine before I found mine.

An actor we work with met a girl while he was making a public appearance on an aircraft carrier. He lost track of her in about ten minutes. And yet, because he was so smitten, he somehow managed to track her down in the army, and they are now married.

GREG, I GET IT! By Leslie, age 29

Greg! I get it. I went to this party and I met this guy. We started talking immediately by ourselves, off in a corner. He asked if I was single and seemed pleased when I said I was. Whenever we split up to talk to other people, or to get drinks or whatever, he always kept his eye on me. It was really cool. I was all excited and fluttery with that "Oh my God, I think I just met someone!" feeling. He didn't ask for my number, but we know lots of people in common, so I thought he was just playing it cool. He never called me! And you know what? Normally I would call our mutual friends and start fishing and trying to figure out what happened and maybe try to find another way to see him again. But instead, I'm just going to move on! Who cares what his deal is. He's not asking me out, so why should I start obsessing over him? I'm just going to go out tonight and try to meet someone else.

IF YOU DON'T BELIEVE GREG

We did an incredibly unscientific poll where we polled twenty of our male friends (ranging from ages twenty-six to forty-five) who are in serious long-term relationships. Not one of their relationships started with the woman asking them out first. One guy even said that if she had, "It would have spoiled all the fun."

What You Should Have Learned in This Chapter

✓ An excuse is a polite rejection. Men are not afraid of "ruining the friendship."

✓ Don't get tricked into asking him out. If he likes you, he'll do the asking.

✓ If you can find him, then he can find you. If he wants to find you, he will.

✓ Just because you like to lead doesn't mean he wants to dance. Some traditions are born of nature and last through time for a reason.

✓ "Hey, let's meet at so-and-so's party/any bar/friend's house" is not a date. Even if you live in New York.

✓ Men don't forget how much they like you. So put down the phone.

✓ You are good enough to be asked out.

Our Super-Good Really Helpful Workbook

Hey, what's a self-help tome without a workbook? Our chapters will all be so brave and wise that we want to make sure you retain as much of the brilliance as you can. So for all of you who feel the need to get out of your problems and into your crayon box, have at it.

Love,

Greg and Liz

Remember in grade school how they told you not to write in your textbooks? Screw that! Grab a pen and list five reasons why you think you have every right or good reason to call him.

1.
2.
3.
4.
5.

Put the book aside and wait an hour. Or at least ten minutes. Then ask yourself: Do I seem pathetic? Do I sound like someone who doesn't trust my own innate hotness? Yes, you do! Now put your dialing finger away, get out of the house, and go find some fun.

P.S.: You just did a *workbook* exercise about a guy who hasn't even extended to you the energy of a phone call. Why would you want to chase *that* down?

he's just not that into you if he's not calling you

Men know how to use the phone

Oh sure, they say they're busy. They say that they didn't have even a moment in their insanely busy day to pick up the phone. It was just *that crazy*. Bullshit. With the advent of cell phones and speed dialing it is almost impossible *not* to call you. Sometimes I call people from my pants pocket when I don't even mean to. We may try to make you think differently, but we men are just like you. We like taking a break from our generally mundane day to talk to someone we like. It makes us happy. And we like to be happy. Just like you. If I were into you, you would be the bright spot in my horribly busy day. Which would be a day that I would never be too busy to call you.

he's just not that into you

The "But He's Been Traveling a Lot" Excuse

Dear Greg,

I recently started dating a very nice man. He's gentle, he's affectionate, he's attentive. It recently became a long-distance thing because of his work. The first problem is, he really doesn't call me when he says he's going to. Actually, he really doesn't call me that much at all. A week will go by, and then I'll call him, and then he'll call me back four or five days later. But then when he does get me on the phone, it's all "honey" and "baby" and "I miss you so much" and "when do I get to see you again?" Is he just not that into me, or can I just chalk it up to the crazy-long-distance thing?

Gina

FROM THE DESK OF GREG

Hey, Crazy Long Distance!

The only distance that's bothering me is the very long distance between you and reality. (Okay, that was a little mean.) Example? In your second sentence you said, "He's gentle, he's affectionate, he's attentive." But a few sentences later you say, "He really doesn't call me when he says he's going to. Actually, he really doesn't call me that much at all." That is neither affectionate nor attentive. And it's not gentle—it's a harsh clanging bell that rings, "I'm just not that into you." Why, then, is he nice when he calls, you ask?

24

Because men are cowards and they would rather wait until the end of time than give you bad news. For the record, a man who likes you wants to spend time with you. And he'll only settle for talking to you on the phone five times a day when he physically can't get on a plane to come see you.

Don't let the "honeys" and "babys" fool you. His sweet nothings are exactly that. They are much easier to say than "I'm just not that into you." Remember, actions speak louder than "There's no cell reception where I am right now."

The "But He's Got a Lot on His Mind" Excuse

Dear Greg,

On New Year's Day, a guy I'd had a few dates with, who I was very excited about, was late for a date. I called him, and he, very apologetically, told me he had to go out of town to take care of his mother. He totally forgot to call me. I'm so confused. His mother is really sick, but it wasn't a desperate emergency; he just had to drive out to Connecticut. Greg, I really like this guy. Please say a sick mother is a good enough excuse to forgive him, and believe he still can be into me.

Bobbie

FROM THE DESK OF GREG

Dear New Year,

Ah yes, here's a bad excuse in sick mother's clothing. Because still, no matter what, what he's telling you is, "You're not on my mind." Because if you were, he would have called you expressing great regret at not being able to spend the day with you. If he had the time to pack and travel, he had the time to call you, and he chose not to. (You call it "forget." I call it "chose not to.") When you like someone, they don't just slip your mind. Especially on New Year's Day. I know it may seem like he had a good excuse, but sadly, I think your New Year started off with a big glass of "He's just not that into you." Now nurse your hangover and find someone who won't forget to call you.

The big question here is, "Is it okay for a guy to forget to call me?" I'm saying to you, "No." Barring disaster—someone had to be rushed to the hospital, he was just fired from his job, someone keyed his Ferrari (kidding)—he should never forget to call you. If I like you, I don't forget you, ever. *Don't you want the guy who'll forget about all the other things in his life before he forgets about you?*

The "He Just Says Things He Doesn't Mean" Excuse

Dear Greg,

I'm dating this guy who ends conversations saying he'll call me at a certain time. Like, "I'll call you over the weekend." Or "I'll give you a call tomorrow." Or if he has to take a call on the other line, he promises, "I'll call you back in a few minutes." And then he doesn't. He always ends up calling, but almost never when he said he would. Should I read something into this, or should I just know to ignore whatever he says when he's getting off the phone with me?

Annie

FROM THE DESK OF GREG

Dear Call Waiting,

Yes, you should read something into it. In fact the very something is "He's just not that into you." Here's the deal. Most guys will say what they think you want to hear at the end of a date or a phone call, rather than nothing at all. Some guys are lying, some guys really mean it. Here's how you can tell the difference: *You know they mean it when they actually do what they said they were going to do.* Here's something else to think about: Calling when you say you're going to is the very first brick in the house you are building of love and trust. If he can't lay this one stupid brick down, you ain't never gonna to have a house, baby. And it's cold outside.

We have become a sloppy bunch of people. We say things we don't mean. We make promises we don't keep. "I'll call you." "Let's get together." We know we won't. On the Human Interaction Stock Exchange, our words have lost almost all their value. And the spiral continues, as we now don't even expect people to keep their word; in fact we might even be embarrassed to point out to the dirty liar that they never did what they said they'd do. So if a guy you're dating doesn't call when he says he's going to, why should that be such a big deal? Because you should be dating a man who's at least as good as his word.

The "Maybe We're Just Different" Excuse

Dear Greg,

I live with my boyfriend who doesn't like to talk on the phone. So when he goes out of town, he won't call me—even to let me know that he got there safely. He just won't call me. He goes out of town fairly often for business. We fight about it all the time. Sometimes I think that our styles are just different, and I'm going to have to learn how to compromise. But then I think that if you're into someone, you would want to call them and talk to them while you're away from them. Am I crazy?

Rachel

FROM THE DESK OF GREG

Dear Not Crazy,

Unless you are dating a spy, this behavior is unwarranted. I travel for a living and find that I call my lady three or four times a day. However, sometimes because of time differences we don't connect. But I will, and she will, always leave a message. I have to say, as a guy I never liked being told to call, which my wife really never does, and that's why I call her as often as I do. We have no rules about calling, but we like and love each other to the degree that we want to talk daily, if not hourly. Listen, I do think space in a relationship is good. Missing someone is a sign of a healthy relationship. Not respecting your need to have some form of connection with him while he's away is not. Regardless of his dislike for talking on the phone, he should respect and care for you enough to call you, if only because he knows that it will make you happy.

Yes, it seems like it's just a machine that transmits voice waves over wires and comes in different styles, like cordless, cellular, handheld, and rotary, but the truth is, the phone has officially reached a new high in relationship symbolism. Is a phone call just a phone call, or is it really the almighty representation of how much he really cares about you? Probably somewhere in the middle. And a good man will know that and use this handy telecommunication device accordingly. E-mails need not apply.

The "But He's Very Important" Excuse

Dear Greg,

You're dumb. A guy who I'm going out with (who I asked out, Greg, by the way) is totally important and totally busy. He's a music video director and travels and has long shoots and lots and lots of responsibilities. Sometimes when he's working, I don't hear from him for days and days. He's really busy, Greg! Some guys are just really, really busy! Don't you ever have really, really busy days? I've learned to live with it and not give him any shit, because I know that's the price I pay for going out with someone really successful and hot and busy. Why are you telling these women to be so needy?!

Nikki

Dear Nikki,

Good to hear from you again. Well, not really. Listen, Nikki. Really busy is another way to say "just not that into you." Totally important is another way to say, "you're unimportant." How great that you've "landed" someone that even you think is out of your league. Too busy and important to ask you out or call you—what a catch. Congratulations on your quasi-relationship! It must feel amazing to know that you've been programmed into the super hot and important busy guy's cell phone, even if he never uses it to call you. You must be the envy of every woman he's really dating.

I'm about to make a wild, extreme, and severe relationship rule: The word "busy" is a load of crap and is most often used by assholes. The word "busy" is the relationship Weapon of Mass Destruction. It seems like a good excuse, but in fact, in every silo you uncover, all you're going to find is a man who didn't care enough to call. Remember: Men are never too busy to get what they want.

IT'S SO SIMPLE

Sadly, I can't be with you ladies all the time, fending off all the bad excuses, and, thereby, bad men that come your way. But what I can do is paint you a picture of what you'll never see when you're with a guy who's really into you: You'll never see *you* staring maniacally at your phone, willing it to ring. You'll never see you ruining an evening with friends because you're calling for your messages every fifteen seconds. You'll never see you hating yourself for calling him when you know you shouldn't have. What you *will* see is you being treated so well that no phone antics will be necessary. You'll be too busy being adored.

HERE'S WHY THIS ONE IS HARD, by Liz

We're smart. We get it. We know guys should be attentive and considerate and thoughtful. I mean, for God's sake, we're not *idiots*. We know that they should call us when they say they're going to and let us know that they're thinking about us. Duh.

But somehow, just when I think I have that lesson perfectly drummed into that thick skull of mine, I meet the one guy who really does have the perfect excuse for being a flake. His family really *is* falling apart and he's the one that has to take care of them all. He really *is* moving and didn't know how difficult it was going to be. He really *does* have that big case at work and can't be around for a while, but he really does—really, really—like me. And I like him so damn much that I'm willing to be patient and cut him some slack and see how it all turns out.

I know intellectually what I'm supposed to be getting from a relationship. I'm writing a damn book about it. But when faced with being offered less than that (sometimes a lot less than that), it's hard to know exactly when to cut loose and move on. He forgets to call me one night—am I supposed to just dump him? He forgets to call me three times—is that when I dump him? It's not easy to find someone you like and are excited about. And you always want to believe that the men you do meet are honest and kind and have your best interests at heart. And when you see the first glimmer of potentially bad behavior, you first hope more than anything that it's not what you think it is. And you want to make sure you don't overreact, punishing him unjustly for some other guy's mistakes. It's a very complicated and tricky world we live in when we choose to date, and I can't keep calling Greg all the time and asking him what I should do.

So right now I'm just trying to notice when a guy's behavior starts making me feel bad about myself—when I start feeling like he's making me suffer. A little pang of disappointment because he didn't call when he said he would? Well, that's okay; we'll see how it goes. A constant state of uneasiness because he's completely unreliable? That's bad. Tears? Really bad. Meeting someone you like and dating him is supposed to make you feel better, not worse. That's always a good rule to live by, no matter what the special circumstances (i.e., excuses) are. It's not easy. But let's try to remember that the next incredible guy we meet with the really good excuse is just another guy who's hurting our feelings.

THIS IS WHAT IT SHOULD LOOK LIKE, by Liz 👤

When I was working with Greg on this book in New York, I noticed that Greg would often call his wife just to tell her that he couldn't really talk to her right then, but he was thinking of her and would call later. It didn't look like the most difficult thing in the world, but it sure seemed nice.

GREG, I GET IT! By Traci, age 25

Greg, I get it! I had two dates with a guy. On the second date we slept together. He said he would call me the next day (Tuesday) and he didn't call me until the weekend. When he called, I told him that it was too late. He was stunned, but really, I don't have time for that shit. It was the first time I had ever done anything like that and it felt great!

IF YOU DON'T BELIEVE GREG

100% of men polled said they've never been too busy to call a woman they were really into. As one fine man said, "A man has got to have his priorities."

What You Should Have Learned in This Chapter

✓ If he's not calling you, it's because you are not on his mind.

✓ If he creates expectations for you, and then doesn't follow through on little things, he will do the same for big things. Be aware of this and realize that he's okay with disappointing you.

✓ Don't be with someone who doesn't do what they say they're going to do.

✓ If he's choosing not to make a simple effort that would put you at ease and bring harmony to a recurring fight, then he doesn't respect your feelings and needs.

✓ "Busy" is another word for "asshole." "Asshole" is another word for the guy you're dating.

✓ You deserve a fucking phone call.

Our Super-Good Really Helpful Workbook

We all love multiple choice. Here's hopefully an easy one for you:

A guy you went out with once and slept with hasn't called you in two weeks. Do you:

a. jump to the conclusion that he's just really busy, lost your phone number, and was struck in the skull, and is now suffering from short-term memory loss, and you should call him?

b. quit your job, stay at home, call the telephone company to make sure your phone works, and wait for him to call?

c. realize he's just not that into you and move on with your life?

Good for you. You answered C. We knew it was easy—but doesn't it feel good to make the right choice?

he's just not that into you if he's not dating you

"Hanging out" is not dating

Oh, there seem to be so many variations to dating, particularly in the early stages of a relationship. So many gray, murky areas of vagueness, mystery, and no questions asked. Dudes love this time because that's when they get to pretend they're not really dating you. Then they also get to pretend they're not really responsible for your feelings. When you ask someone out on a real bonafide date, you're making it official: I'd like to see you alone to find out if we have a romantic future together (or at least pretend to listen to you while I ponder whether you're wearing a thong). In case you need more clues: There's usually a public excursion, a meal, and some hand-holding involved.

The "He Just Got Out of a Relationship" Excuse

Dear Greg,

I'm really, really in love. I want to say that first. I've been sleeping with a really, really good friend of mine who recently got out of a terrible marriage. Because he is in the process of going through a very traumatic breakup, he's really clear that he can't have any kind of expectations or demands put on him in any way. Basically, he wants to come and go as he pleases. We've been seeing each other and sleeping together for six months now. It's very painful not to be able to have any say about when or how often I get to see him. Yet it's also very painful to think about not being with him. I don't like being in this powerless a position, but I feel like if I hold out, eventually he'll be mine. But it's very difficult for me in the meantime. What should I do?

Lisa

Dear Really Really,

Let's talk about Johnny Really Good Friend and your Johnny Really Great Friendship. It sure works out well for him. Because you were a pal during his disaster of a marriage, he will always be able to play the "friend" card with you. He only has to be responsible for the expectations of a friend, rather than the far greater expectations of a boyfriend. After all, being a "pal," you wouldn't want to put him through any more emotional turmoil while he's going through his "very traumatic breakup." He's got the ultimate situation: a great friend with all the benefits of a girlfriend, whom he can see or not see whenever he wants to. He may be one of your closest friends, but I'm sorry to say, as a boyfriend, he's just not that into you.

Beware of the word "friend." It can often be used by men or the women that love them to excuse the most unfriendly behavior. Personally, when I'm picking friends, I like the ones who don't make me cry myself to sleep.

The "But We Really Are Dating" Excuse

Dear Greg,

I've been dating a guy for three months. We spend four or five nights a week together. We go to events together. He calls me when he says he's going to and never flakes out on me. We're having a great time. He recently informed me that he doesn't want to be anyone's boyfriend and isn't ready for a serious relationship. But I know he's not dating anyone else. I think he's just scared of the term "boyfriend." Greg, I'm always hearing that women should listen to men's actions, not their words. So doesn't that mean I should just ignore him and be secure in the fact that he wants to spend all this time with me—that no matter what he's actually saying, the truth is he's really into me?

Keisha

Dear Not Listening,

I looked up "I don't want to be your boyfriend" in the Relationship Dictionary, just to make sure I wasn't mistaken, but I was right. It still means "I don't want to be your boyfriend." Wow. And this is coming from a guy who's spending four or five nights a week with you. That must hurt. Nice to know your not-boyfriend gets to live in your world commitment-free. Not quite sure what you're getting. If you want to give all that time to a guy who's proclaiming he's not your boyfriend, then go ahead. But I'd hope you'd at least go find someone who wasn't saying to your face, "I'm just not that into you."

Men, just like women, want to feel emotionally protected when a relationship starts to become serious. One way they do that is by laying claim to it. They actually want to say "I'm your boyfriend" or "I'd like to be your boyfriend" or "If you ever break up with that other guy who's not your boyfriend, I'd like to be your boyfriend." A man who's really into you is going to want you all to himself. And why wouldn't he, hot stuff?

The "It's Better Than Nothing" Excuse

Dear Greg,

I've been dating a guy for six months. We see each other about every two weeks. We have a great time, we have sex, it's all really nice. I thought if I just let things develop, we would start to see each other more often. But instead, it's staying in this every-two-weeks situation. I really like him, so I still feel like it's better than nothing. And you never know, things can change at any time. I know he's really busy, and maybe this is the most time he can dedicate to a relationship right now. So maybe I should actually feel honored that he's able to give me as much time as he does, and he might actually really like me. No?

Lydia

FROM THE DESK OF GREG

Dear Better Than Nothing,

Really? Is better than nothing what we're going for now? I was hoping for at least a lot better than nothing. Or perhaps even something. Have you lost your marbles? Why should you feel honored for getting scraps of his time? Just because he's busy doesn't make him more valuable. "Busy" does not mean "better." In my book, any guy who can wait two weeks to see you, is just not that into you.

Oh, how easy it is for you all to forget what it's about! Let me remind you: It's about the guy who wants you, calls you, makes you feel sexy and desired fully. He wants to see you more and more often because every time he sees you, he likes and then loves you more and more. I know. Every two weeks, once a month, seeing someone, having a little love and affection may help you get through the day or the week or the month—but will it help you get through a lifetime?

The "But He's out of Town a Lot" Excuse

Dear Greg,

I've been seeing this guy for about four months. He goes out of town a lot, so we're just doing this casual thing. But then we'll start spending some consistent time together, and just when I get up the nerve to have a "talk" about where the relationship is going, he has to leave town again. I feel stupid talking to him about things when he's just about to leave town. But when he gets back, I feel stupid bringing it up when we haven't seen each other in a while. It's hard for me to broach this subject—we have such a nice time together that I don't want to ruin it with a "relationship" talk.

Marissa

FROM THE DESK OF GREG

Dear Time Traveler,

Here's the little secret about some guys who travel: They look forward to leaving. They quite like having the frequent flier miles and the built-in escape hatch. It's hard to hit a moving target. There are ways to travel and be in a relationship, and there are ways to travel and make sure you stay out of one. The easy way to know the difference is if the guy tells you all the time how bummed he is that he has to keep leaving you. If he is not making a serious effort to make sure that while he's out of town you don't go out and find

41

someone else, then I think you've just boarded the he's-just-not-into-you jet. Buckle up.

You have every right to know what's going on between you and someone you're knocking socks with. And the more confident you are that you deserve that (and much more), the more you'll be able to ask your big questions in a way that won't feel heavy and dramatic, I guarantee you.

IT'S SO SIMPLE

From this moment on, right now, as you read this, make this solemn vow about your future romantic relationships: no more murky, no more gray, no more unidentified, and no more undeclared. And if at all possible, try to know someone as best you can before you get naked with them.

HERE'S WHY THIS ONE IS HARD, by Liz

I hate talking about my feelings. I hate talking about my "relationship." I know I'm a chick and chicks are supposed to be all emotional, but I'm not. I don't like it one bit. I particularly don't like asking a guy where the relationship is going or how he feels about me. Ew. It should be natural and easy and obvious.

So I guess if I have to start thinking and planning and devising all sorts of ways to find out what kind of situation I'm in, I'm probably not in that good a situation. Shit.

But wait. Starting a new relationship is terrifying. We are all old enough to have experienced or witnessed the triage of broken romance. We know that if there has been a beginning to a relationship, there has been, if we are still out there dating, always an end to the relationship. And the endings always suck.

So of course people, women included, will create all sorts of tricks and diversions and distractions to try to not notice that we might in fact be getting into a relationship. That just seems like a very crafty and understandable aspect to human nature. So what if in the beginning or a while into it, it's a little vague? Who wants to be that crazy girl who needs to know exactly what is going on the minute she meets a guy? You want to be the cool girl—the girl who knows how to hang out and not be all demanding. That's who I always wanted to be. That's who I always was.

The thing about that cool girl is that she still gets her feelings hurt. She still has reactions to how she's being treated. She still hopes he'll call, wonders when she'll get to see him again, and if he's excited about being with her. I hate that.

Maybe this is just me, because my priorities have changed as I've gotten older. But now I don't want to be "sort of dating" someone. I don't want to be "kinda hanging out" with someone. I don't want to spend a lot of energy suppressing all my feelings so I appear uninvolved. I want to be involved. I want to be sleeping with someone I know I'll see again because they've already demonstrated to me that they're trustworthy and honorable—and into me. Sure, in the beginning you have to be somewhat cautious about how much you give away. But that caution shouldn't be to make *them* feel more comfortable; it should be because you know that you are ultimately a delicate, valuable creature who should be careful and discerning about who gets your affection. That's what I'm doing now. And it's not going so badly.

THIS IS WHAT IT SHOULD LOOK LIKE, by Greg 🕴

My friend Mike liked my friend Laura. After band practice he asked her out and now they're married. My friend Russell met this girl Amy and they dated and got married. My friend Jeff met a girl out of town and went and visited her the next weekend and never stopped visiting her until he moved in with her. It's really that simple. *It's almost always that simple.*

💡 GREG, I GET IT! By Corinna, age 35

I was dating a guy for a couple of months when it suddenly dawned on me that he didn't seem particularly excited about me. In the past, that would have made me try harder, make excuses for it, and even confront him with it. Instead I did a little experiment. I assumed he just wasn't that into me and I stopped calling him. As I suspected, he never called me again! I can't believe how much time I saved just by recognizing that I was the one doing all the work, and that I wanted more!

IF YOU DON'T BELIEVE GREG

100% of guys polled said "a fear of intimacy" has never stopped them from getting into a relationship. One guy even remarked, "Fear of intimacy is an urban myth." Another guy said, "That's just what we say to girls when we're just not that into them."

What You Should Have Learned in This Chapter

✓ Guys tell you how they feel even if you refuse to listen or believe them. "I don't want to be in a serious relationship" truly means "I don't want to be in a serious relationship with you" or "I'm not sure that you're the one." (Sorry.)

✓ Better than nothing is not good enough for you!

✓ If you don't know where the relationship is going, it's okay to pull over and ask.

✓ Murky? Not good.

✓ There's a guy out there who will want to tell everyone that he's your boyfriend. Quit goofing around and go find him.

Our Super-Good Really Helpful Workbook

It's very easy for us to give advice, and quite honestly, it's kind of fun. We've even learned a little about ourselves in the process. (Well, at least Liz has.) Why don't you give it a try? It's fun to feel you know better than other people!

Dear Pretty Girl who bought this book (that's you),

I have been dating this guy for a couple of months. However, I've never actually been on an official date with him. He always tells me to meet him somewhere, like a bar or a friend's house. He doesn't seem like he wants to spend time alone with me unless we're having sex. I like having sex with him—so can't I keep doing that until he gets to know me better and realizes he's really into me?

Answer:

If you've answered this successfully (which means you've told this lovely lady to get rid of Booty Call the Barfly and go find herself a man that can at least spring for a slice of pizza), then you know your brain knows how to solve these problems; you have this information inside of you, and probably always have. It's just a lot easier to see it when it's not you. And now that you've been reminded, you can use your rediscovered wisdom for your own benefit.

he's just not that into you if he's not having sex with you

*When men like you,
they want to touch you, always*

Ladies, you are going to meet, and have already met, many, many men in the years that constitute your dating lifespan. And I hate to tell you this, but some of these men will simply not be attracted to you. I know you're hot, but that's just the way it is. (Even Cindy Crawford has dudes that go, "I don't know what the big deal is all about.") And every single one of these men that are not attracted to you will *never ever tell you that*. Oh, the things they'll say . . . they're scared, hurt, tired, injured, sick, scared (again). But the truth is simple, brutal, and clear as a bell: He's not attracted to you and doesn't want to hurt your feelings. If he were into you, he would be having a hard time keeping his paws off you. Oh the simplicity of it all! If a man is not trying to undress you, he's not into you.

The "He's Afraid to Get Hurt Again" Excuse

Dear Greg,

I had a boyfriend ten years ago. I bumped into him on the street recently, after not having seen him for many years, and we start "dating" again, even though it is unclear if that's exactly what's going on. He won't kiss me or make a pass at me. But, Greg, we're going salsa dancing, we're going barhopping, we're staying out late, talking and dancing and laughing and flirting. He keeps telling me how great I look, how great it is to see me. One night he even told me he loved me and hoped I'd always be in his life. My friends all say he's just afraid to get hurt again and I should stick this one out. He's a great guy. Doesn't he seem really into me, but he's scared? Salsa dancing, Greg, till four in the morning. Salsa dancing. Please advise.

Nicole

FROM THE DESK OF GREG

Hey Salsa,

I'm a dude. If I like you, I kiss you. And then I think about what you look like in and out of your underwear. I'm a guy. That's how it works. No ifs, no ands, and clearly no buts. Is he scared? Yes, he's scared of hurting your feelings. That's why he hasn't clarified the relationship. He may even be biding his time hoping he will develop deeper feelings for you. When this dude tells you he loves you and that he hopes you never lose touch again, he may as well be signing your yearbook. He loves you as a friend. If he were *in* love with you, he wouldn't be able to help himself from getting involved in a romantic relationship regardless of his fear or past experiences. I say, move on! Go meet someone more worthy of your affections and hot salsa moves.

There are lots of reasons a man might not want to take a friendship to the "next level." It really doesn't matter what they are or if they make any sense to you. The bottom line is that when he imagines being with you more intimately (and trust me, we do think about these things), he pauses and then says to himself, "Nah." Don't spend any more time thinking about it, other than saying to yourself, "His loss."

The "He's So Into Me That Now He's Not" Excuse

Dear Greg,

I've been dating a guy for a month. We've had sex and it's been nice. Just when it seemed like things were really "taking off," we stopped having sex. I've stayed over at his house four times now and we end up just...sleeping. Some cuddling, but that's about it. It's weird, but sex just doesn't happen anymore. It's humiliating to have to ask him what's going on, so I'm just going to assume that it's actually because he's really, really into me, and he's just scared.

Sally

Dear Just Cuddling,

A month? A month?! Are you freaking kidding me? This should be the time when he's getting comfortable enough to bring up the subject of outfits, positions, lotions, and anal. A month? The only thing he should be tired of is thinking of different ways to ravage you. And after only a month, he really wouldn't be tired of that. Now, you can get up the nerve to ask him what's going on—communication is never a bad idea. But my guess is that you probably already have your answer. I say start walking, and let him explain to your hot ass why he doesn't want to have sex with you. And if he doesn't, well, you know what we'd say to that.

Ahh, here comes the big "fear of intimacy" debate. Is there such a thing? Many, many people are in therapy for it, a lot of self-help books are dedicated to it, a lot of shitty behavior is excused because of it. (We even took a poll about it just a few pages ago.) Sure, many people have been hurt in their past, and now have a fear of intimacy. But guess what? If a man is really into you, nothing will stop him from being with you—including a fear of intimacy. He may run and get his butt into therapy if there's some serious problem, but he'll never keep you in the dark.

The "But It Still Feels So Good" Excuse

Dear Greg,

I'm dating this guy who told me after the first date that he can't be monogamous. He doesn't believe in it.

I slept with him anyway. Then I realized it would be bad to date him, so I told him I couldn't go out with him. But then I missed him. So now we're doing this weird thing where we hang out, go on dates, and then have these little "sleepovers." I sleep over at his house and we just cuddle. It's so nice, Greg. We make dinner, watch television, laugh. It's really sweet and I feel so close to him. He doesn't try anything and we just enjoy each other's company. I know I'm not supposed to expect anything more, but I'm feeling like his girlfriend, and you never know where this could lead. It feels so great to stay over and wake up with him! Is there anything wrong with this?

Pat

Dear Slumber Party,

Let me see. It wasn't hard enough for you to hear that the person you are dating doesn't want to be monogamous. But then you slathered on the extra hurt by continuing to see him while he may be sleeping with other people. So now you're feeling like his girlfriend, but without any of the perks. Not even sex. What kind of weird science experiment are you doing with your emotions? Don't get me wrong, Madame Curie—I know it's nice to have companionship and wake up with somebody that you really like, but that's what pets are for. Pets are God's way of saying, "Don't lower the bar because you're lonely." Clearly you know yourself well enough to know that you aren't cool with sharing your man, and by the way . . . you shouldn't be cool with it! You deserve a boyfriend of your very own who you feel safe enough to have sex with.

The old-fashioned idea is that women withhold sex when they want power. It seems like men can play that game too. Why buy the cow when you can get the intimacy for free? Oh, it's so simple. If a guy is happy lying around in bed with you eating cookies and watching old movies, and he's not gay, then he's just not that into you.

The "Multiple Excuses" Excuse

Dear Greg,

My boyfriend of a year and a half doesn't seem attracted to me. He doesn't want to have sex that often, maybe once every other week. Often I have to initiate it. When I ask him about it, he tells me that he's really stressed about work, but that he really is attracted to me. Before that he told me it was because his mother had recently died and he was too depressed. But when I really think about it, it's been pretty much like this ever since we met. Maybe for the first couple of weeks I felt like he thought I was hot, but since then he has never really seemed that into me physically. I love him, and it's the most loving and healthy relationship in every other way, but now I spend a lot of time feeling frustrated and unattractive. My friends say I should believe what he's saying. But I'm starting to feel like he's just not that into me, physically.

Dara

FROM THE DESK OF GREG

Dear Let's Get Physical,

If I'm really into somebody, I want to put it in them. And then take it out. And then put it back in them later on. So when we're picking someone who we want to spend a lot of time with, even perhaps the rest of our lives, we generally try to pick someone who likes to do the things we like to do. Including, if not especially, sex. You can accept his excuses all you want, but you have to ask yourself, is this the relationship you want to be in? Is this how you want to live the rest of your sex life? He may be into you, he may not, but the only thing you have to answer is, is this how you want to feel, perhaps forever?

The Egyptians painted pots about it, the yogis write books about it, the Jews have made religious laws about it. They all believe that one of the strongest ingredients to a healthy union is sex. One of the great joys in life is that you get to have sex. The last person who should be stopping you from enjoying that is the person you're dating.

IT'S SO SIMPLE

Learn it, live it, like it, love it: If a man likes you, he's going to want to have sex with you. Sure, things may slow down in a long-term relationship, but even then, it's a joy, a gift, and your right to have a fantastic sex life.

HERE'S WHY THIS ONE IS HARD, by Liz

Well, duh. It's about sex. Talking about sex. Asking about sex. Asking for sex. Jeez. That's really fun. And I don't know about you, but I would much rather believe, any day of the week, that a man is too scared, too stressed, too sad, too spiritual, too angry, too fat, too crazy, too in love with his ex-girlfriend, too scared, too sensitive, too sunburned, too in love with his mother, too homicidal, too *anything*, than find out that he's really just not attracted to me. Or that he doesn't want to have sex with me because then it will mean we're in a real relationship, and actually he doesn't really like me that much. It's extra confusing because we're talking about sex (embarrassing) mixed with emotions (mortifying) mixed with our own insecurities (nightmare). And in the case of long-term relationships, people always tell you the sex goes away anyway, so what does it really matter if it goes away a little sooner than you wanted it to? Isn't the other stuff much more important, like being compatible and him being a good person and potentially a great father?

Because it's such a psychologically complex issue and talking about it is so excruciating, I would almost be able to settle for the relationship with the guy who only likes sleepovers, or the boyfriend with the presumed low sex drive. I mean, he still enjoys my company. I might be able to sleep next to the guy who has stopped wanting to have sex with me, without saying a peep. Or keep dating the guy who seems to want to be my boyfriend but doesn't seem to have any interest in ever seeing me naked. I might even be able to exist in a peaceful marriage with a wonderful man who is more like a best friend than a husband.

If it wasn't for those goddamn happy couples I know.

And I'm not talking about the ones you see on the streets slobbering all over each other. Who knows what they're like behind closed doors. I'm talking about my friends who I know quite well, who manage to juggle work, careers, intimacy, even kids, and still manage to have sexy, loving relationships. I could easily settle for less if I happened to be the type of person, upon seeing these couples, who just thought, *What's the big deal about* that? But I'm not that person. I'm the type of person who looks at them and says, "Damn. That's what I want." It's really a bitch. That means I have to be the type of girl who is going to ask the guys the mortifying questions, and worse, who might break up with a really great guy if he just doesn't want to have sex with me enough or at all. But all I can say is that I suffer from the affliction of believing I can have a wonderful man love me and be wildly attracted to me. I also believe that when that wanes, as it naturally will, we can both make it a priority to try to stay wildly attracted to each other. If you suffer from that affliction as well, you better pull the pillow out from under Mr. Sleepover and take away his cookies and milk. We deserve more than a slumber party.

THIS IS WHAT IT SHOULD LOOK LIKE, by Greg

Don't ask me how I know, because I don't want to tell you, but I can assure you that my parents, who are in their seventies, after children, illnesses, aging, stressful jobs, and daily annoyances (read: life), are still having sex. If my parents can do it, so can you and your boyfriend.

GREG, I GET IT! By Dorrie, age 32

I was dating a guy I met on a job. We had to spend a lot of time together and it was really romantic getting to know him and working with him. After the job ended, we'd still get together and go on dates and kiss good night. This went on for two months. He would never take it any farther. But in the meantime I met his family, went to big functions with him, made plans with him. It was like we were seriously dating, but without the sex. I knew he hadn't been in a relationship for a long time, so I thought he was just taking it slow. But then I realized, Greg, after the third month, that he was getting to *feel* intimate with me without actually *being* intimate with me. I got up the nerve to ask him if this was how it was going to continue, and he started blub-bering and stammering about relationships and how scary they are and whatever. I got out of there and fast, because I realized, no matter how nice he was to me, and how intimate we were pretending to be, he was just not that into me and I wanted more.

IF YOU DON'T BELIEVE GREG

Twenty out of the twenty men polled said, without hesitation (well, it was all done by e-mail, but they all seemed really sure about it), that they have never been really into a woman who they didn't want to have sex with. One man wrote in, "What?! Excuse me?! And the point is?!"

What You Should Have Learned in This Chapter

✓ People tell you who they are all the time. When a man says he can't be monogamous, you should believe him.

✓ Companionship is wonderful, but companionship with sex is even better. Call a spade a spade or, more fittingly, a friend a friend, and go find yourself a friend that can't keep his hands off you.

✓ Your lost self-esteem may take longer to find than a new boyfriend, so prioritize accordingly.

✓ If you're tempted to spend countless nights just cuddling with someone, buy a puppy.

✓ There's someone out there that *does* want to have sex with you, hot stuff.

Our Super-Good Really Helpful Workbook

Get a bright red crayon. Color in this flag. You've just made a big red flag.

Good, because that's what a man not wanting to have sex with you is. Now put down the crayon and go get yourself some good loving.

he's just not that into you if he's having sex with someone else

There's never going to be a good excuse for cheating

If he cheats on you, throw the deadbeat out. Just kidding. I know things aren't that simple. This is a very complicated subject, I'll admit. Some will argue, "It's just sex, what does it matter?" Some will argue that you shouldn't throw away a meaningful relationship just because of one indiscretion. This all may be true. But this is what I know: Whatever problems you may have been having in your relationship, they didn't merit him having sex with someone else. Don't ask what you did wrong. Don't share the blame. And in case he tells you that it just "happened," please remember, cheating doesn't just "happen." It's not an accident as in, "Oops, I just slipped and fell into a sexual relationship with someone else." It was planned and executed with the full knowledge that it could end your relationship. Know this: If he's sleeping with someone else without your knowledge or encouragement, he is not only behaving like a man who's just not that into you, he's behaving like a man who doesn't even like you all that much.

The "He's Got No Excuse and He Knows It" Excuse

Dear Greg,

I have been living with my boyfriend for a year. I recently found out that about a month ago he slept with someone he worked with, twice. (The girl told me at a party!) I confronted my boyfriend and he confessed. I packed my things and moved to a friend's. He's now calling me constantly, begging me to give him a second chance. He says he doesn't know why he did it, but promises he'll never do it again. He really feels bad about it. What should I do?

Fiona

FROM THE DESK OF GREG

Dear A Month Ago,

Let's see. He slept with someone else while he was living with you, and you only found out because the *girl* told you about it. Sounds like a winner. When's the wedding?

Seriously, let's talk about that special month in your home. In that month, he had sex with someone else twice, came back, and slept in the same bed with you. He was actively hiding this secret from you every time he looked into your eyes. And let's remember, this gentleman didn't confess by his own volition—Skanky the Homewrecker did it for him. So, if he had his way, this lovely month of dishonesty would have turned into two months, three months . . . forever. Do all his apologies count for something? Well, you can choose to believe he is sorry. You can choose to believe he will change. But in my book, lying, cheating, hiding is the exact opposite of the behavior of a man who's really into you.

Cheating is bad. Not knowing why you cheated is even worse. If one red flag isn't enough for you, how about two? Don't date any man who doesn't know why he does things.

The "But I've Gotten Fat" Excuse

Dear Greg,
I had been dating a guy for about two years, and I thought things were going really well. After he came home from a family visit, he told me he slept with someone he met at a bar. I was devastated and asked him why he did it. He told me I had put on some weight and therefore he wasn't that attracted to me anymore. I'm confused. He's right. I have put on about twenty pounds. Should I break up with him or start going to the gym?

Beth

Dear Twenty Pounds,

I definitely think you should lose 175 pounds—in the form of your loser boyfriend—not the twenty that you're talking about. He just cheated on you and called you fat. How many low-self-esteem protein shakes can one person drink? Using your weight as an excuse for his cheating is not only mean, but simply not valid. If he has a problem with anything in your relationship, he's supposed to talk to you about it, not put-his-penis-in-a-strange-vagina about it. And by the way, how's he going to react if you ever get pregnant or grow older and get a few wrinkles? Or wear a color he doesn't like? Get rid of this loser or I'm going to come to your house and get rid of him for you.

The "He Has a Stronger Sex Drive Than I" Excuse

Dear Greg,

I have been dating a guy for a year. I found out through a friend that he has been sleeping with someone I sort of know. I confronted him, and he told me that I don't give him enough sex and that's why he's been sleeping around. He's right. Sometimes I don't want to have sex when he wants to. It's not all the time, but he definitely does want sex more often than I do. So, in a way, he's right. Should I just forgive him and try to put out more?

Lorraine

Dear Putting Out,

The only thing you should be putting out is any of his clothes that are still in your house. There is no excuse for him sleeping around. Period. There are so many ways to deal with the truly common problem of differing sex drives within a relationship. Usually one would start with an adult conversation wherein a discussion ensues that hopefully resolves with the two parties agreeing to work on it—not him jumping in the sack with *someone you know*! Not only does he not respect you or the relationship, he doesn't respect himself enough to be in a meaningful relationship. This isn't even a question of "he's just not that into you." In this situation, if you like yourself at all, you should definitely not be into him.

These last two guys are good. They've betrayed their relationships and humiliated their girlfriends. Then they tell them that it's their fault, knowing that they have just done something that has so demoralized them that they will be their most inclined to believe a load of horse crap. If something is wrong in a relationship, here's a bright, mature idea: Talk about it. Don't let any man blame you for their infidelity. Ever.

The "But at Least He Knew Her" Excuse

Dear Greg,

I've been going out with a guy for about a year. We are in love and get along great. Recently he met with his ex-wife who he hasn't seen in about a year. (She had left him because she met someone else.) They have been divorced about two years. They slept together. I am very upset and want to break up with him. He wants me to forgive him because it wasn't like it was someone new; it was his ex-wife. He promises me that it will never happen again—just old feelings came up and he couldn't control himself. I want to forgive him—it was only once—but it feels like everything is ruined. Can he really be in love with me and do this to me?

Joyce

FROM THE DESK OF GREG

Dear Ruined,

Who decided to put the "ex" in "sex"? You're telling me that the "get out of her vagina free" card is that he used to be married to her? Does that mean he can also sleep with the woman who cleans his teeth? How about the lady who develops his photos? Hope he's not going to his high school reunion. Again, it doesn't really matter if he's still in love with you. He's given you a pretty big clue about how he feels about your relationship. The bigger question is, can you still be in love with him?

You can't blame a guy for having feelings. You love someone, you break up, you still have feelings. Thank God for that really. But having feelings doesn't mean you have to have sex. That required him to take his feelings and use them to be some-where alone with his beloved, undress her, kiss her, and do all the other things involved with having sexual intercourse with someone. Hooray for feelings. Just keep them in your pants.

IT'S SO SIMPLE

If you are in a mutually established monogamous relationship, then when someone cheats on you, they have decided to blatantly disrespect a very important decision you two made together. They've chosen to do this without your knowledge, thereby adding lies and secrecy to your relationship.

Let's call cheating what it is: a complete betrayal of trust. Cheaters are people who have a lot of stuff to work out and they're working it out on your time and with your heart. Some cheaters might give you an excuse, some might not have one at all, some might even blame you. No one can tell you exactly what to do when faced with this very complicated and painful situation. But the bottom line is, is this what you had hoped for in a relationship?

THIS IS WHAT'S HARD ABOUT THIS ONE, by Liz

In my life, I have had two men tell me that they had slept with someone else, in the beginning stages of our relationship. (In one case, it came to me in a dream, literally, and I confronted him. *That* really freaked him out.) Anyway, both times what I got from it was that these men wanted me to know that they could never be trusted. They were barely in the relationship and had already pulled the escape hatch.

The beginning of two people getting together is such a fragile, tender time. There's nothing like a big pail of Sleeping with Someone Else to put out the fires of a budding relation-ship. I personally would never be able to overcome that. So this isn't really a tough one for me. Now, if I use my imagination, I could see that in the beginning, the lines are not that clearly drawn, the rules aren't that firmly in place yet. Maybe it *is* the last fling before the final commitment. If it's early in the relationship, it can be hard to know if the guy is just getting something out of his system and it's a one-time thing, or if it's a guy who's just a big jerk. That's the thing about dating—you're having intimate experiences with someone who, at the end of the day, you don't know very well. You don't know his personal code of honor, you don't have his dating rap sheet. You have to go by instinct, how much you care about him, and what he has to say for himself about it. All I can think is, how sad to be having *that* conversa-tion in the beginning of things, when everything is supposed to be cozy and snugly and people are usually on their best behavior. If nothing else, I wish better for us all. I really do.

THIS IS WHAT IT SHOULD LOOK LIKE, by Liz

A friend of mine told a story about a date with a guy she was really excited about: He stood her up. He then called her, begging her forgiveness and giving some excuse. She told him to get lost, telling him that he only gets one shot with her, and he blew it.

Imagine what this woman would have done with a boyfriend who cheated on her?

P.S.: One could say she cleared the path for the next guy, who didn't blow it and is now married to her and treats her like a queen.

GREG, I GET IT! By Adele, age 26

I was dating a guy I really liked who played in a popular local band. After a few weeks of dating he told me that he slept with some girl after one of his gigs. Sadly, a few years ago I probably would have been so into dating a guy in a band that I would have just pretended it had never happened and forgotten he had ever told me about it. This time, I told him that it was cool; he's allowed to do whatever he wants. He just won't be seeing me ever again. It felt great!

IF YOU DON'T BELIEVE GREG

100% of guys polled said they have never accidentally slept with anyone. (But many of them wanted to know how this accident could occur, and how they can get involved in such an accident.)

What You Should Have Learned in This Chapter

✓ There is no excuse for cheating. Let me say it again. There is no excuse for cheating. Now you say it. There is no excuse for cheating.

✓ Your only responsibility in someone else's lapse in judgment is to yourself.

✓ Cheating is cheating. It doesn't matter whom it was with or how many times it happened.

✓ Cheating gets easier every time it's done. It's only hard the first time, when one feels the sting of morality and the guilt of betraying someone's trust.

✓ Cheaters never prosper. (Because they suck.)

✓ A cheater only cheats himself, because he doesn't get to be with *you*.

Our Super-Good Really Helpful Workbook

Here are our five suggestions on what your man could have done if he was unsatisfied in your relationship. (You'll notice, none of them include sleeping with someone else.)

1. Talk about it.
2. Write about it.
3. Sing about it.
4. E-mail about it.
5. Even put on a puppet show about it.

Now think of five of your own. (We know we took the easiest ones, but we still think there's at least five more you can come up with.)

1.

2.

3.

4.

5.

Read them, have a laugh, dump the cheater. Of course I can't tell you what to do. But dump him.

6

he's just not that into you if he only wants to see you when he's drunk

If he likes you, he'll want to see you when his judgment isn't impaired

It's really fun to drink and date. Who doesn't like to bring booze to the make-out party? It can make you more confident, and let's face it, confidence is a rush and you are more likely to talk dirty. It's all good, as long as you don't confuse ice-breaking for real intimacy. Being drunk or high is an altered state that can actually take you away from real feelings. Be aware that if Boozy the Clown has to slip on the red nose every time things get intimate, it could be symptomatic of a bigger problem.

The "But I Like Him This Way" Excuse

Dear Greg,

You're so dumb. My boyfriend, the music video guy? He really likes to drink. He has a really hard job and needs to unwind. And when he's drunk he's really affectionate and tells me all these great things about how he feels about me. I think that's great! Some people need alcohol to get the courage to share their feelings and I don't think there's anything wrong with that! In fact I don't think there's anything wrong with drinking a lot after work. It's fun. It's like a party all the time. He doesn't miss work. He's just a bad boy. I like bad boys. They're exciting. If you don't, you're too uptight.

Nikki

Dear Nikki,

Nikki, Nikki, I know you think he's so hot. You love that drunky "Oh baby, you're so beautiful" slurry thing he does when he's at the bar, or maybe even that cute rendition of "I love you so much you're the best thing that ever happened to me, babe" while he slings his arm around you a little too hard. I can see how his inebriated, sweaty proclamations of love can make you feel all warm inside. Nikki, you must know this by now: You can't believe everything a guy says when he's drunk. And take it from a former bad boy: "Bad Boys" are bad because they're troubled, as in having little self-respect, lots of pent-up anger, loads of self-loathing, complete lack of faith in any kind of loving relationship, but yes, really cool clothes and often a great car. Just the kind of guy for you, right, Nikki?

Ladies, don't let your desire to be loved and feel affection cloud your judgment (like a big tall glass of scotch). If you are lucky enough not to be dealing with the profound, painful problems of being married to, living with, or born to, an alcoholic, and you just happen to be dating a guy that you notice drinks an awful lot, please beware. Know you deserve not just an affectionate, attentive boyfriend, but you deserve an affectionate, attentive, sober one.

The "At Least It's Not the Hard Stuff" Excuse

Dear Greg,

My boyfriend is a lawyer and happens to smoke pot every night. When he does, he acts and talks just like he does when he's sober. I guess it's weird that he's always high and I'm not, but it doesn't seem to be an issue with us. My friends think it's weird that I'm dating a pothead. But it's not like he's really acting like a pothead, so what does it matter? I can't imagine how this has anything to do with how into me he is or not. Right?

Shirley

Dear High Times,

Wrong! Let's take a quick health ed class on what pot does to the brain. Smoking pot makes your brain work slower, and makes you less in tune with your surroundings and more introverted. It dulls your senses and clouds and impairs your sense of reality. So, he's always stoned when he's with you. That really means he likes you more when there's less of you. You're going out with someone that doesn't enjoy you at your full levels. That's tantamount to him liking you better when you're in the other room. This doesn't mean that he's not into you. It just means that he likes his pot better than you. By the way, if he ever got arrested for pot, he most likely would lose his license, because criminals are not allowed to be officers of the court. So at least you're in good company, because he likes pot better than his job, too!

Don't be fooled. Don't let the guy who's not falling down drunk and peeing in his pants get away with the fact that he is quietly, more gracefully, bombed out of his mind every single moment he's with you. It's still inebriation, it's still checking out, and it's still not good enough for you.

IT'S SO SIMPLE

Sometimes life is incredibly difficult and painful. If you're looking for a partner to share your life with, it's better to pick someone who's able to meet it headlong with his full faculties.

Extra note to the ladies: If you happen to notice an increase in *your* drinking or smoking while with Mr. Party Man, please be aware. This is not an "if you can't beat it, get drunk with it" situation. Your getting drunk won't make *him* seem any less of a drinker.

HERE'S WHY THIS ONE IS HARD, by Liz

I don't know why, but I've dated a lot of alcoholics. Or as I would have probably said at the time, "guys who like to drink a lot." I really don't know why. There isn't alcoholism anywhere in my family. I'm not a big drinker myself. I think I just always thought they were *fun*. I loved when my boyfriend climbed the water tower at my friend's roof party wedding while he was bombed out of his mind and exposed himself to everyone. I thought it was hilarious. And when that guy, drunk, lit a pack of firecrackers in his kitchen just to make me laugh? Well, that was adorable. I found it particularly amusing when my boyfriend disappeared for a week and, after a lot of calling, I found out he moved back in with his ex-girlfriend.

I think there are probably personality traits that many alcoholics share that happen to be the traits that I find really attractive. The drunks I've dated were all spontaneous, funny, passionate, smart, creative, emotionally unavailable, unreliable, insensitive, dishonest, and slightly abusive. How I loved them all.

74

So what's hard about this one? Nothing much. Except, boy, does alcohol factor in a lot in the beginning stages of dating. The first kiss, the first time having sex . . . most relationships would never get off the ground without a couple of glasses of wine first, and there ain't nothing wrong with that. I've dated recovered alcoholics as well, and jeez, having to do those first big moments without a drop of liquor? Well, it's tough. But actually . . . kind of great as well. Romance translates very well into sober.

So we all have to be clear about the difference between a couple of drinks to relax, and constant substance abuse. Okay. Got it. And Greg wants to make sure we don't date any of the alcoholics or drug addicts we might meet along the way. I think that's fair, don't you?

Okay, Greg. We won't. We promise.

THIS IS WHAT IT SHOULD LOOK LIKE, by Liz

I know a successful businessman who used to get stoned every single night, and sometimes in the morning too. He dated women who didn't like it, and he would try to cut down while he was dating them. One day he met the woman of his dreams and she would have none of it. He stopped cold turkey and now spends his days completely sober and very happy with it.

GREG, I GET IT! By Nessa, age 38

I started dating a guy I really liked. We met at a party when we were drunk, and we hooked up a little. Then we were dating, and I was so nervous around him (because I liked him so much) that I drank more than I normally did. He likes to drink too, so I was also just trying to keep up with him. Finally I realized that we were getting drunk at some point every time we saw each other. Normally I would just stay quiet and see how it all turned out, but this time I got up the nerve to say something. He listened to me and agreed to have a "sober" date. It was awkward at first, but then awesome. I'm so glad I had the courage to speak up!

IF YOU DON'T BELIEVE GREG

100% of men polled said they have never vomited in the bed of a woman they were really into. (Apparently these guys don't know how to have a good time.)

What You Should Have Learned in This Chapter

✓ It doesn't count unless he says it when he's sober. An "I Love You" (or any semblance thereof) while under the influence of anything stronger than grape juice won't hold up in court or in life.

✓ Drinking and drug use are not a path to one's innermost feelings. Otherwise people wouldn't smash empty beer cans against their skulls or stick their fingers in fire to see if they can feel anything.

✓ If he only wants to see you, talk to you, have sex with you, etc., when he's inebriated, it ain't love—it's sport.

✓ Bad boys are actually bad.

✓ You deserve to be with someone who doesn't have to get loaded to be around you.

Our Super-Good Really Helpful Workbook

There's often a lot of drinking during the early stages of a relationship. It may be hard to first even notice that you actually haven't ever seen your dude sober. Or, then figure out if it's a problem (for *you*). So we've just made you a little calendar. (You can fill in your own dates.) Shade the clown nose for every day you see him intoxicated. (That includes pot, muscle relaxers, whippets, Oxycontin, Xanax, and too much Red Bull.) Only you can decide what's too much or too little for you. But at least you'll have the clown's habits in front of you in black and white.

S   M   T   W   T   F   S

he's just not that into you if he doesn't want to marry you

Love cures commitment-phobia

Just remember this. Every man you have ever dated who has said he doesn't want to get married or doesn't believe in marriage, or has "issues" with marriage, will, rest assured, someday be married. It just will never be with you. Because he's not really saying he doesn't want to get married. He's saying he doesn't want to get married *to you*. There is nothing wrong with wanting to get married. You shouldn't feel ashamed, needy, or "unliberated" for wanting that. So make sure from the start that you pick a guy who shares your views for the future, and if not, move on as quickly as you can. Big plans require big action.

The "Things Are Really Tight Right Now" Excuse

Dear Greg,

I have a boyfriend who I've been living with for three years. I'm about to turn thirty-nine, and I have started bringing up the idea of long-term plans, like, say, marriage. He always seems open to it, but then talks about how bad his finances are. He's an investment banker who works for himself, and he lost a *lot* of money in the past two years, a lot of clients, as well, and his business really has gone down the tubes. He says he's under a lot of pressure. Am I being unreasonable to want to know where this is all going? Please let me know.

Barbara

Dear Pressure Cooker,

Definitely do not say a word. Keep very, very quiet. Maybe you should even think about moving into another apartment so you'll be out of the way during this oh-so-important time. Don't forget he's the Most Important Man in the World and his business is failing and that means everything to everybody. What the heck are you thinking, lady? Of course you should know where it's all going. Do you not value yourself and your time? Certainly three years invested earns you the right to know what your future holds. Any investment banker worth his salt would agree with me.

Everyone lost money over the past two years; the stock market crashed and the economy has been in the toilet, and yet imagine—many have still managed to get married. If you are both in your late thirties, and you've been dating for three years, and he's not begging you to be his wife, you might want to take this stock tip: Mr. Dow Jones is just not that into you.

There will never be a good time, financially, to get married, unless you're Shaq or Ray Romano. But somehow people manage. If your man is using money as an excuse not to marry you, it's your relationship that's insecure, not his bank account.

The "He's So Terribly Put Upon" Excuse

Dear Greg,

My boyfriend is fairly rich—not Donald Trump, but he has family money, and he's a successful businessman on his own. He feels that for all his adult life, women have looked at him like a meal ticket. As soon as they've been dating for a couple of months, he says he feels the "marriage vibe" start happening. I'm not like that. I work. I support myself. I never take money from him. I just love him. I'm thirty-five and we've been dating for three years now, living together for two. We never talk about it. Ever. From what I've gathered about his history, he seems to always break up with women soon after they start asking him about marriage. But he must know I'm different. I know having money must be weird, so I'm trying to be understanding. Can the fear of being taken advantage of really be that strong? Or should we start suspecting he might not be that into me?

Arlene

Dear You're So Money and You Don't Even Know It,

Wow. So now having *too much* money is being used as an excuse not to get married. What will you crazy kids think up next? Again, at the risk of repeating myself: You are allowed to have aspirations for your future and to know whether the relationship you're in is going to take you closer to those aspirations or be the demise of them. No amount of money in the world can buy that away from you. If you're afraid to even broach the topic of marriage for fear that he's going to break up with you, then this dude not only has all the money, but all the power as well. And, well, that just pisses me off personally, because no one should be that lucky. Don't be intimidated by his big heaps of cash or his big heaps of baggage of past relationships. Find out if Mr. Moneybags is really into you for the long haul, and don't take any of his Poor Little Rich Boy excuses.

I personally think if you have to sit and figure out what's the best way to bring up the idea of marriage to someone whom you have been intimate with for a substantial amount of time, it's not good news. Most guys, or let's say the guys I want you to be dating, will make sure, as soon as reasonably possible, that you know they mean business. So if he's not, get to his mixed feelings and conflict as fast as you can. Then, as soon as you're ready, go find someone that is spending time worrying about how *you're* feeling.

The "Is This Really an Excuse?" Dilemma

Dear Greg,

I'm thirty-three and have been living with a guy for two years. We are in love, he's great to me, and we get along perfectly. He has no problems committing to me—he just doesn't want to get married. He married young and got divorced young. He says he doesn't want to ruin a good thing. It seems insane of me to break up with him because he doesn't want to get married. We are sharing a life together and are very happy. He's even open to having kids. He just doesn't want to get married. In this case, I don't think he's just not that into me. I think he's just not that into marriage.

Lindsey

Dear Common Law Lady,

Okay, this may be controversial, but I'm going to say it. No matter how traumatic a divorce was (and I know they can be traumatic in epic proportions), the person you plan on spending your life and having children with should love you enough to get over it if getting married is important to you. Only you can decide if marriage is a deal breaker for you. I can't tell you if it's worth breaking up with him if you're happy and have a nice life together. That's for you to decide. I have never been divorced, I'll give you that, but I'd marry my wife in every time zone if that's what she wanted. In my very conventional opinion, I believe one foot in is the same as one foot out.

Marriage is a tradition that has been somewhat imposed on us, and therefore has a lot of critics. Be that as it may, if someone is as against marriage as you are for it, please make sure there aren't other things going on besides he's just not that into the institution.

The Age-Old "He's Just Not Ready" Excuse

Dear Greg,

I've been dating a guy since I was twenty-three. I'm twenty-eight now. We started talking about marriage two years ago, and he said he wasn't ready. So we moved in together to help him get "ready." We talked about it recently and he said that he still wasn't ready. He reminded me that we're young and we still have a lot of time and there's no need to rush. In a way, he's right. I'm only twenty-eight and people get married much later these days. And sometimes it takes longer for guys to grow up than girls. So I want to be understanding, but I'm just not sure how long I'm supposed to wait. Does he need more time or is he just not that into marrying me?

Danielle

Dear Waiting at the Altar,

He's right. Why rush? It's only been five years. He's going to know you so much better after ten. And you have all the time in the world, right? You know, in case after ten years he decides he's *still* not ready. I hate to tell you this, but here's why he feels rushed: He's still not sure you're the one. Yep, my lovely, I know it's hard to hear, but better to hear it now than ten years from now. So you can stay with him and continue to audition for the part of his lucky wife, or you can go find someone who doesn't need a decade or two to realize you're the best thing that ever happened to him.

I'm not ready. This is the most often used excuse in the world, but it always seems to do the trick. Women love waiting around for men to be ready. You women must enjoy it, because you do it so much of the time. Which is ironic to me, since you're the ones with the biological clocks that are supposedly ticking away. Listen, we all know that couple who's been dating for five years . . . eight years and still hasn't gotten married. We know it never works out well for that couple. So how about you stop waiting—and start looking for that guy who can't wait to love you.

The "He Just Needs a Better Role Model" Excuse

Dear Greg,

You're so dumb. My boyfriend, you know, the music video director? He says he doesn't believe in marriage. But I know it's because of his freaking crazy mother (she's he's just not that into you

insane, Greg) and his parents' totally psycho marriage. I'm so ignoring him because I know he's going to figure out soon enough that I'm not his mother and he will some day ask me to marry him. Besides, I'm not ready for marriage right now, anyway.

Nikki

FROM THE DESK OF GREG

Dear Nikki,

It's a shame you're not ready to marry Mr. Music Video Spielberg, because you guys seem to have all the building blocks of a great and lasting relationship. But seriously, I love guys that tell their women unequivocally that they don't believe in marriage. I mean, it's not like they're giving anyone a hint or anything. Listen, Nikki. This guy isn't walking down the aisle anytime soon unless he's picking up an MTV Music Video Award. But feel free to keep reminding him that you're not his mother. In fact, make sure you nag him about it repeatedly, over and over again. He'll really love that.

It's a really big deal for a good guy to finally meet the woman he wants to spend the rest of his life with. Chances are, if he truly knows it, he's not going to immediately tell her that the idea of legally spending the rest of their lives together is repugnant to him. I'm just saying.

IT'S SO SIMPLE

What's the big, nasty, awful shame, ladies? It's okay to want to get married. And it's okay to ask someone if they see themselves being married, or if they see themselves being married to you. Let me remind you: There are many, many men out there who want to be and are getting married; that's why there are so many florists, priests, and taffeta-makers out there.

P.S.: Don't spend your time on and give your heart to any guy who makes you wonder about *anything* related to his feelings for you.

HERE'S WHY THIS ONE IS HARD, by Liz

A lot of people think marriage is bullshit. A lot of women, men, philosophers, anthropologists, psychologists, feminists, and scientists all think, for different reasons, that marriage is a deeply flawed, outdated institution built for failure. Toss a quarter anywhere and it will hit someone who'll be happy to tell you something bad about marriage.

So there's all *that*. But is that what we're really talking about here? I don't think so. I think that sometimes men want you to think that's what the debate is about. But let's be clear. The question at hand is only this: Is he making lame transparent excuses about marriage to cover for the fact that he really doesn't ever see a future with you?

That's the hard question. And women are smart. If they really got quiet and stopped listening to the excuses, or believing what they wanted to be true and what they hope he's really saying, and just got all centered about it, I think women would always know. They'll always know the difference between a man who truly has issues with marriage but is deeply committed to the relationship and them, and a guy who's just being a weenie.

But this is what's hard about this one. It's very easy to feel stupid about wanting to get married, particularly when you're with someone who doesn't. I mean, you two are so happy together—why rock the boat? It's just like you're married, so what's the big deal? What do you care what your family thinks—are *they* living with you? Just because all your friends are getting married, does that mean you have to? Jeez, it sounds like you don't care who you marry. You just want to *be* married.

These are really good points. And let's face it, marriage hasn't gotten a lot of good press in the past four decades. And some women, frankly, really *don't* care who they marry and just want to be married. But again, that's not what we're talking about. Before you enter into the sociopolitical-anthropological debate about marriage as an antiquated financial contract, blah, blah, blah, ask yourself some very serious questions. Questions that only you can answer in your most sane, clear-headed of moments: Do you feel truly loved? Do you feel he is deeply committed to you? Do you feel he has any doubts about wanting to build a life with you? If the answer to these questions are yes, yes, no, then let the debating begin, because he might have a point. But if you feel that he's always holding something back, or that you're spending a lot of energy trying to change yourself into something you think will make him happier, then divorce yourself from him and move on. Don't let him make you feel stupid about wanting to feel loved.

THIS IS WHAT IT SHOULD LOOK LIKE, by Liz

I have a lady friend whose boyfriend had just moved cross country to live with her, and we were all out having drinks. We got on the subject of marriage, and he went on a huge diatribe of how he didn't believe in marriage. He grew up in an environment where there was crazy pressure to get married, and all he saw were unhappy, unhealthy marriages. My friend was surprised by this strong reaction, and fairly upset about it. She wasn't an intensely marriage-minded gal, but she always thought it was going to be an option. She gave it a good deal of thought and realized that what she really wanted was just to be with this man, who had just moved his entire life to be with her. So she got used to the idea that she would never be married. A year later he proposed, because he realized he was in love with her and knew it was something that was important to her.

GREG, I GET IT! By Sandy, age 33

I was dating this guy for a year and a half. We'd had a few conversations about marriage. One day I realized that all the conversations we'd had about marriage were started by me. "Sure," he always replied, "you are my soul mate. I'm so passionate about you. I love you more than I've ever loved anyone, blah, blah, blah." When I'd asked him flat out, "Do you want to marry me?" he'd say, "Yeah, I would like to." Then it dawned on me—I had never heard the words "I want to marry you" come out of *his* mouth. Literally, the day I had this revelation, I dumped him. Needless to say, I'm so much happier now dating guys who in the first week say, "Wow, I can't believe you're not married. You're great."

IF YOU DON'T BELIEVE GREG

100% of the guys polled told us they would have no problem marrying a woman who they were positive was the love of their life. One man answered, "What kind of knucklehead has a problem marrying the love of his life?"

What You Should Have Learned in This Chapter

✓ "Doesn't want to get married" and "Doesn't want to get married to me" are very different things. Be sure about which category he falls under.

✓ If you have different views about marriage, what else are you not on the same page about? Time to take inventory.

✓ If you don't feel like you're rushing, why are you waiting?

✓ Nikki is crazy.

✓ There's a guy out there who wants to marry you.

Our Super-Good Really Helpful Workbook

Please write down how long it took you to start thinking that you might want to marry the guy you're dating.

Write down how long it took you to know for sure.

Look and see if these seemed like a reasonably appropriate amount of time. Then tell yourself that he has no good excuse for not having figured that out by now too.

he's just not that into you if he's breaking up with you

"I don't want to go out with you" means just that

Everyone wants to be loved and needed, particularly by the person who just broke up with us. I understand. What could be better than hearing from the man who just told you he didn't want you in his life anymore, his sad, wistful "I miss you so much" voice on the other end of the phone? It's validating. It's exciting. It's irresistible. But resist you must. If he's not calling you to tell you he hired a U-Haul to come pick up all your stuff and move it back into his house, then consider yourself a nice, downy little pillow cushioning him from his feelings of loneliness and loss that he's not fully ready to deal with on his own.

The "But He Misses Me" Excuse

Dear Greg,

My boyfriend and I had been dating for two years, living together for one. We started fighting and having all sorts of problems. He broke up with me three weeks ago and I moved out. Of course, I'm devastated. The thing is, he calls me all the time. He wants to chat. He asks about my friends, and wants to know how my family is. He likes to keep up with the little details of my life, just as if we were going out. My friends all say I should stop talking to him, but I think he misses me, and I like that. I miss him. I feel if I stay in touch with him, it will remind him of how great I am, and eventually he will realize that we should be together again. What do you think?

Brenda

FROM THE DESK OF GREG

Dear Misty Water Colored Memories,

So glad he likes to keep up with the Way You Were. Who doesn't need another phone pal, especially since you have a new phone and a new apartment? Put him on hold and listen to me, missy: A man who wants to make a relationship work will move mountains to keep the woman he loves. If he's not calling you to tell you he loves you and wants you back, it should only be because he's showing up at your new residence to do it in person. If he's not trying to romance your socks off with dates, flowers, and poetry, it should only be because he's too engrossed with his couples counseling workbooks and is prioritizing getting back on the right track. If he's not doing any of that, he may love you, he may miss you, but ultimately he's just not that into you. Stop taking his calls and let him really know what it's like to live without you.

Don't be flattered that he misses you. He *should* miss you. You're deeply missable. However, he's still the same person who just broke up with you. Remember, the only reason he can miss you is because he's choosing, every day, not to be with you.

The "But It Really Takes the Pressure off of Us" Excuse

Dear Greg,

I was seeing a guy for about a month. He broke up with me, saying that he didn't feel like it could be something serious. I understood and took it well. He wanted to know if we could still hang out as friends. I said sure. Now we get together and go out and then come back to his place and have sex, just like we did before. (But now, we're "broken up.") He's really, really cute and I love having sex with him. I also think he must like me if he can't stop being around me. And I think it's kinda cool—all the pressure's off and we're having a great time together. I've decided that I think it's fine and I'm not going to

call his attention to the fact that we're actually dating. Except for the fact that we broke up.

Cheryl Lynn

FROM THE DESK OF GREG

Dear Breaking Up Is Easy to Do,
  My God, this guy is brilliant. He goes out with you, dates
you, breaks up with you, then continues to sleep with you,
which basically absolves him of all responsibility toward
your feelings. After all, you're not going out anymore. It's
genius! It's diabolical! He should be writing a book, not us! In
fact, I bet this guy could get his own little cult going if he
wanted to. And let me guess, you'd be happy to sign up for
that as well. For the record, this guy doesn't "like you so
much that he can't stop being around you." Because here's
what guys don't do if they can't live without you: They don't
break up with you. This guy is so seriously not into you, it's
crazy. The only way you're going to figure out how into you
you are, is how fast you get rid of him.

It's very tempting when you really want to be with someone to settle for much, much less—even a vague, pathetic
facsimile of less—than you would have ever imagined. Ladies,
please, keep your eye on the prize. Remember always what
you set out to get, and please don't settle for less. If you can't
do it for you, do it for everyone else: These guys are able to
exist because there are a lot of women out there who allow
them to.

The "But Everyone Is Doing It" Excuse

Dear Greg,

Yes. Breakup sex. It's been hot. Emotional. Amazing. I'm tortured and I love him and I can't stop myself. I thought that you were allowed breakup sex, but now I'm in over my head. Help.

Ileen

•FROM THE DESK OF GREG

Dear If You Know Better, Why Are You Still at His Apartment?

Hey, girl. Put down the penis, put your clothes back on, and go directly to your best friend's house. Do not find an excuse to stay. Do not think that because of all the crazy hotness of it all, it now means that you're meant to be together. Yes, breakup sex does seem like a good idea, because, hey, it's nice to have sex with someone you know. And it's nice to have sex with someone you have all these dramatic feelings about. It makes it all, well, *dramatic*. But now you know. It confuses everything and makes you feel like crap, because face it, you're a woman, and women can't separate sex and emotions. (How many times will you make me have to say that? I sound like such a jerk!) So now you don't ever have to make that mistake again. Got it? He's not into you. He's into the very-bad-idea-that-masquerades-as-a-good-idea, breakup sex. Over and *out*.

Don't underestimate the power of sex, even with someone you've been doing it with for a very long time. Especially with someone you've been doing it with for a very long time. Breaking up means not seeing them again, which also implies not seeing them naked again. It may be tempting to forget this pearl of wisdom, but just remember, it's still called breakup sex. No one has yet to rename it oh-my-God-the-sex-was-so-good-we-got-back-together-again-and-lived-happily-ever-after sex.

The "But Then He Wants to Get Back Together" Excuse

Dear Greg,

I have a boyfriend who keeps breaking up with me. He also keeps calling me and begging me to get back together with him, each time telling me that he misses me so much and has made a terrible mistake. He's done this three times now, every six months. I hate it, but I keep taking him back because I love him. I keep telling myself that he must be really into me, if he keeps coming back—right?

Christina

FROM THE DESK OF GREG

Dear Yo-Yo Champion,

Funny how you notice how many times your dude comes crawling back to you, while I notice how many times he's told you that he doesn't ever want to see you ever again. For both of us the number is three, but I'll put money down that the breakup count isn't over yet. Because sadly this is what that guy is doing during your relationship recess: He's sniffing around for something better, and when he doesn't find it, he gets lonely and comes "home." It's not that he's so into you. It's that he's so not into being alone. Don't give him the chance to break up with you for the fourth time. (God, even the idea of it sounds beneath you, doesn't it?) Reset your breakup maximum to one and move on.

Deciding to get back together with someone is a complicated and difficult decision. Just remember that the person you are getting back together with is the same person who, not long before, looked you in your beautiful face, took full stock of you and all your qualities, and told you that he was no longer in need of your company. If aliens haven't recently abducted your beloved and switched his brain for the brain of a guy who's really into you, please consider the option that the bum maybe just got a little lonely.

The "But I'm So Damn Nice" Excuse

Dear Greg,
My boyfriend and I broke up a week ago. (He broke up with me.) He's going out of town to see his mother, who's having an operation, and I volunteered to take care of his two cats, who I love. He accepted. I think he was really impressed and touched that I'm handling it so well.

My friends think I'm a wimp, but I think they're being small. We had been together for three years—it's not like I'm suddenly not going to care about him or his cats (who are adorable).

Dana

Dear Cat Lady,

Don't even try it. I'm onto you. If he hasn't figured out after three years that you're the woman who will make his life heaven right here on earth, a couple of tins of cat food aren't going to do the trick. So how about when he returns from helping his mother with her operation, you surgically remove *him* from *your* life? Hand over his house keys and the number of the pet boarding place that has the nicest ad in the yellow pages. Doing anything above and beyond those measures won't reinstate you as his girlfriend. It will make you his maid.

Don't confuse being classy with being a doormat. Classy is walking away with your head held high, graciously, and with dignity. Being a doormat is offering to drive him to the dentist for his root canal.

The "I Do Not Accept His Breakup" Excuse

Dear Greg,

Okay, so my music video boyfriend dumped me because he's an asshole, but now I have some of his stuff in my apartment and I'm not going to give it back because I know he's going to change his mind, and I keep calling him and calling him to try to get him to change his mind, which I know he will, because I know he really does love me and he doesn't mean this, but all he wants is his stupid Palm Pilot back. A guy doesn't say all the nice things he said to me and take me to all the cool parties he took me to and introduce me to all his cool friends and then just suddenly change his mind. People don't just totally, totally like someone one day and then wake up and not want to be with them the next. I'm so completely devastated because I really, really loved him. You might not believe me, Greg, but I really did love him and I loved being with him and now I can't even get out of bed 'cause I've been crying so much. He's just in a bad mood and I'm not going to believe him.

Nikki

FROM THE DESK OF GREG

Dear Nikki,

I'm sorry you got dumped. Can't say I didn't see it coming, but now's not the time to gloat. What you need to do

immediately is turn down the psychotic. Calling him inces-
santly and holding his stuff ransom is really no way to win
a man back. In fact that's the best way to elicit the "What did
I ever see in that psycho bitch?" response. Whatever happened to that super-confident, strong-willed woman? Has
she been reduced to a groveling lunatic? No she hasn't, so
cut it out, Nikki. Sometimes people change their minds,
sometimes they meet someone else, sometimes they get
sober (he was drinking excessively), and sometimes he was
just a jerk who you're lucky to be rid of (not that I was judg-
ing). It doesn't matter, because you cannot change his mind.
Oh, Nikki, please behave, because what will really haunt you
later is not losing the excessive-drinker-who-didn't-ever-
want-to-get-married-and-was-too-busy-and-self-important-
for-you, but how you behaved during the breakup. I swear.

One simple rule, ladies: Always be classy. Never be crazy.
Okay, actually it's two simple rules, but trust me, you will
never be sad you followed them. If for no other reason, it will
ensure that you never have that awful memory of cutting his
clothes in half or dumping his dog on the side of the road.

IT'S SO SIMPLE

A guy says he doesn't want to be with you. Sometimes that guy realizes he's made the biggest mistake of his life. And then sometimes he doesn't. Either way, *either way,* your only job is to move on with your life, and fast. He can always try to chase you down as you're running down the block. If he does, just remember that it will sound like this: "Let's get back together." "Let's go into counseling." "Let's try again." "I miss you. I made a mistake. I want to be with you." Here's what it won't sound like: "Will you walk my dog?" "Just calling to check in." "Want to see that movie?" "Will you go to Cousin George's wedding with me?"

HERE'S WHAT'S HARD ABOUT THIS ONE, by Liz

Oh, I don't know, how about loving someone and being with them and knowing their family and friends and every inch of their body and seeing them naked every day and never having felt this way before and feeling like your whole life has changed for the better and compiling hours and days and weeks of happy memories and thinking you'll spend the rest of your life together and then finding out that in fact he doesn't even want to see you . . . tomorrow.

And so is it so wrong to wait around looking for a glimmer, a ray, a sign of hope from him that perhaps he has second thoughts about it? That perhaps he has come to his senses and realized you were the best thing that ever happened to him, that no one will ever be as good to him as you were, that he won't find anyone whom he can connect with on such a deep and profound level and who understands him as much as you do? Is that so wrong? Is it so wrong to continue to talk to him, see him, bake him cookies, buy him presents, burn him CDs, feed his fish, talk to his parents, call up his friends, break into his voice mail . . . just kidding. But seriously, is it so wrong to handle a breakup in a classy, mature, loving manner, where you keep in contact and talk and remain friendly and perhaps go to the movies on occasion? And would it be so terrible if perhaps the by-product of that classy mature behavior is that he comes to his senses and realizes you were the best thing that ever happened to him? Would that be so terrible?

I don't think so. I think it's a smart, scrappy plan that shows a fine combination of wile and maturity. I can't believe that in the history of mankind and breakups, it has never ever worked. What is wrong with these men?

Fine. Breakups, I've heard, are supposed to be just that. Breaks. Hard, clean breaks. No talking, no seeing, no touching . . . keep your hands to yourself. The relationship is over. Half the people I know move after a huge breakup, and frankly that makes perfect sense to me. Again, for the most part, we kind of know this. You're not supposed to sleep with the guy who just broke your heart a week ago. Fine. But what are we supposed to do instead? How are we going to fill our time if we're not trying to win him back (while we keep trying to convince our friends that we're really not), huh?

Fine. Next time I'm in this situation I'll cry. Stay in bed and wail. Go to the gym if I can. Call all my friends and burden them with my misery. Sleep too much. Cry some more. See my therapist more often. Get a puppy. Do whatever I have to so eventually I can move on.

Fine. Have it your way, Greg. I still think my way could work.

THIS IS WHAT IT SHOULD LOOK LIKE, by Liz

I know a couple who dated for many years and then broke up. They had a lot of mutual friends and everyone took it very hard. Five years later, they got back together again and are now happily married. During the time apart, there were no dates or phone calls or being chums. They didn't torture, confuse, or hurt each other in the process. They moved on with their lives, grew up separately, and only then realized, much later, that they could be together again.

GREG, I GET IT! By Callie, age 26

Recently I told my ex-boyfriend that I had started dating someone. We had been broken up for six months. Now I can't get rid of him! He calls me, reminds me I have to pick up mail, asks me to go to the movies. I'm not going to lie, I love the attention. But guess what? I now understand that none of it is real. He's not asking to get back together with me. He's just jealous. His behavior might have at one time in my life given me hope, but now it just makes me laugh. Men are so obvious.

IF YOU DON'T BELIEVE GREG

100% of men polled said that when they broke up with someone, it always meant that they didn't want to go out with them anymore.

(One guy even asked, "How can you have great breakup sex if you don't break up?" Don't go out with this guy!)

What You Should Have Learned in This Chapter

✓ You can't talk your way out of a breakup. It is not up for discussion. A breakup is a definitive action, not a democratic one.

✓ Breakup sex still means you're broken up.

✓ Cut him off. Let him miss you.

✓ He doesn't need to be reminded that you're great.

✓ He can take care of his cat.

✓ "Classy" doesn't "break into his answering machine."

✓ There's a guy out there who's going to be really happy that you didn't get back together with your crappy ex-boyfriend.

Our Super-Good Really Helpful Workbook

Oh my God. It's so weird. We found this on the floor when we were writing this book. It's from your future boyfriend. Isn't that a weird coincidence?

> Hey, Hot Stuff,
> Can't wait till you get over that guy you were with. He sounds like a real jerk. Hope it's soon. You're way too tasty to be alone for too long.
> Come find me. I'm out here waiting.
>
> Your Future

9

he's just not that into you if he's disappeared on you

Sometimes you have to get closure all by yourself

He's gone. Poof. Vanished into thin air. Well, there's no mixed message here. He's made it clear that he's so not into you that he couldn't even bother to leave you a Post-it. This time you may not be so quick to make excuses for his behavior. It's so painful, it's impossible not to be hurt or angry. But because of that, you might be tempted to make some excuses for yourself. You have good reason to want to spend a lot of energy solving the Mystery of the Disappearing Man. But all those excuses, however valid they are, will not help you in the long run. Because the only part of that story that's important to remember is that he didn't want to be with you anymore. And he didn't have the guts to tell you that to your face. Case closed.

The "Maybe He's Dead" Excuse

Dear Greg,

 I had a brief fling with a really cute French guy. It was really fun, but it also felt like maybe it could be more than that. He went back to France and we started e-mailing each other. It was really sweet and romantic. All of a sudden, after one of my e-mails, he stopped writing. It's been two weeks. Greg, maybe something happened to him. Maybe he didn't get my last e-mail. Maybe I wrote something that upset him. I hate thinking that I will never ever hear from him again. That's so harsh. Can't I write him again, just to make one more attempt to connect with him?

 Nora

FROM THE DESK OF GREG

Dear Freedom Fry,

 Yes, you can e-mail him if you want to give him the opportunity to reject you one more time. Could he have gotten run over by a *pommes frites* truck and is in the hospital and that's why he disappeared? Yes. But I have to say, the law of averages says that it's more likely he met someone or realized that the long distance thing wasn't for him, or that you simply may not be the American girl of his dreams. If you want to write him and ask him again to close the door in your face, for the .0001%

chance his phone died and his e-mail crashed, and he lost all your contact information, be my guest. Just don't say I didn't warn you.

There's nothing worse than having no answer, in business, friendships, and especially romantic relationships. But the bad news is, no answer is your answer. He may not have written you a good-bye note, but his silence is a deafening "see you later." The only reason to ever write him again is to give him the chance to say it louder, with words. And don't you remember? You're far too busy and popular for that.

The "But Can't I at Least Yell at Him?" Excuse

Dear Greg,
  I was dating a guy seriously for three months when he suddenly disappeared. I didn't hear from him for days. I was worried, so I called his best friend and he told me that my boyfriend got back together with his old girlfriend and moved in with her. I get that he's just not that into me, but don't I have the right to find out how he could do that to me? Don't I have the right to not let him get away with it?

  Renee

Dear Just Walk Away Renee,

Sure. But guess what. He knows you're going to be pissed. He's a colossal asshole, not an idiot. He played the whole thing out in his head. That's why he just disappeared. What he doesn't know is how quickly you can get over him and his bad behavior. You'll show him that by never talking to him, or his friends, ever again.

P.S.: And he's not getting away with anything. Everywhere he goes, he's still that same asshole.

In the short term it might feel good to call someone and yell at him. But in the long run, you will have wished that you had not given him that much credit for ruining your life. Or even your day. Let someone else expend that kind of energy on him. It may feel like you're letting him "get away with something." But trust me, nothing you say is going to be news to him. And you've got much better things to do with your time.

The "But I Just Want an Answer" Excuse

Dear Greg,

I went on a trip with my boyfriend of six months to California. We had a great time. When we got home, he went to visit his family in Boston. When I called him to check in, his mother told me that he had gone to visit his friend in Florida. I never heard from him again. It's devastating. I believe the only way I can honor my feelings and the relationship is to talk to him and find out what happened. What's wrong with that?

Liza

FROM THE DESK OF GREG

Dear You Picked a Lemon,

Do you deserve to know what happened? Yes. But fortunately for you, *I* can tell you what happened. You were dating *the worst person in the world.* What could he possibly say that will make a big happy lightbulb go on over your head and make you exclaim, "Ohhh, *that's* why my boyfriend left me without a word and went to Florida and vanished into thin air"? Nothing he could possibly say will be satisfying to you. But what will be satisfying is if you don't spend another moment of your energy on him. You picked a lemon. Throw it away. Lemonade is overrated.

P.S.: If I ever go to Florida, I'll kick his ass.

Sometimes a person's behavior is so abhorrent that it leaves little doubt as to what to do. The big mistake you made was choosing that person to begin with. The quickest way to rectify that mistake is by learning from that, moving on, and choosing much more wisely in the future. And quick, before any more of your precious time is wasted.

IT'S SO SIMPLE

The reason it's so painful when someone disappears is you have to face the fact that the person you loved had probably left you a long time before he grabbed his coat and scrammed. The hard part is realizing that he was lying to you, in some way, before the moment of vanishing. Don't ask yourself what you did wrong or how you could have done it differently. Don't waste your valuable heart and mind trying to figure out why he did what he did. Or thinking back on all the things he said, and wondering what was the truth and what was the lie. The only thing you need to know is that it's really good news: He's gone. Hallelujah. See ya in the funny papers, yellow-belly!

HERE'S WHY THIS ONE IS HARD, by Liz

Oh, for Pete's sake. This one is *impossible*. He *disappeared*. He just stopped calling you or writing you or seeing you *out of the blue*. You were in what you considered some sort of "relationship." You felt that whatever you had together warranted even the tiniest explanation if one of you decided to call it quits. But instead, there's silence. No explanation, no good-bye. Just a vanishing. There's nothing worse, in dating terms, *nothing worse*, than that sick feeling you get in the pit of your stomach when it looks like the guy you were seeing or getting to know has decided to bail on you instead of talking to you about it. *Nothing worse.*

So first you feel hurt. But *then* you feel helpless, completely and totally helpless. He just disappeared, making you feel like you had absolutely no value or meaning to him whatsoever.

And you might be shocked, too. He might not have ever behaved this way before. So now you're also unbelievably disappointed. "Really? Now I have to not like him? Now I have to think he's a jerk? That's what this relationship added up to? There's got to be some kind of reasonable explanation." So then you start giving this great guy a big heap of your time and energy, making up excuses for why he's disappeared (he's busy, he's busy . . . and maybe he's busy), still hoping that he will come to his senses and at least drop you an e-mail. You then start going through everything you said, did, or wrote that might have driven him away. What was the thing you said that was so inappropriate or needy, that he had no other recourse than to head for the hills? You blame yourself for some perceived strategic misstep. "Oh, if only I had played it better! He would still be mine!" Or simply, you're worried that he's dead on the street somewhere. Why else would he just disappear like that?

So then, you want to call him and say something. Or write him. You're either angry or hurt, or still holding out hope that's he's in a coma at a hospital somewhere. But however you feel, you definitely think it is your right to either yell at him or find out what happened. What's worse than not knowing? Nothing. Except maybe not getting to tell him off.

Greg would say that the best revenge in this situation is not anger, but emotional distance, as quickly as possible. Greg would say that we have the answer. He didn't want to stick around, and wasn't man enough to tell us to our face. Isn't that answer enough? That's when I would say to Greg, "No, actually it's not. That answer's definitely not good enough. I want to know *why*." And then Greg would say,

"Really? Are you sure? Do you really need him to detail every last reason why he didn't feel like seeing you ever again?"

I hate Greg.

Breakups are horrible. But to me, what's truly devastating is to feel like you weren't even worth a breakup. Again, it's natural to want to do something about that. Greg just wants that "something" to be about moving on, as opposed to looking back. Not having closure is one of the most difficult things for me (and many people) to live with, so I know why it might be impossible not to call the cad. But I guess Greg would lecture you again (he's such a know-it-all), and say that before you make that phone call or write that e-mail, you should at least play it out in your head. Will it really make you feel better? Do you think it will really change the way he feels about what he did, or you? Is it the *only* thing you can think of that will help you move on? If it is, then I say to hell with Greg—give the guy a call. But I guess the hope is (for me, at least) that when a guy no longer wants to communicate with me, and doesn't have the manners or courage to tell me that to my face, he's given me all the information I need. It's the toughest one of all to put into practice. But I definitely like the kind of girl who could do it. Good luck to us all!

THIS IS WHAT IT SHOULD LOOK LIKE, by Greg

I regretfully admit to having "disappeared" on a woman in my previous life as a single guy. A year later I saw this woman on the street, standing in front of a café. She looked stunning and was holding hands with a very handsome dude. I realized that I was of course ten million miles out of her head, and probably had been two minutes after I stopped calling her. *Her life looked way more dignified than my behavior.*

GREG, I GET IT! By Liz, age 41

Okay, Greg, I won't e-mail the French guy. I promise.

IF YOU DON'T BELIEVE GREG

100% of men polled who had "disappeared" on a woman said that at the time they were completely aware of what a horrible thing they were doing, and no woman calling them up and talking to them would have changed that.

What You Should Have Learned in This Chapter

✓ He might be lying in the hospital with amnesia, but more likely he's just not that into you.

✓ No answer is your answer.

✓ Don't give him the chance to reject you again.

✓ Let his mother yell at him. You're too busy.

✓ There's no mystery—he's gone and he wasn't good enough for you.

Our Super-Good Really Helpful Workbook

We'd have an exercise if we really thought this guy was worth the time, but he's not. So take the afternoon off and go out and have a good time.

Love, your friends at *He's Just Not That Into You,* Greg and Liz

Okay, if that's not good enough . . .

It's the oldest trick in the book, but it's the only thing we're willing to grant you. Write the guy a really, really long letter, asking him every question you need to. Say everything you want to say. Call him all the names you feel like. Say something mean about his mother. And then—you guessed it—just rip it up.

That's the most time we'll let you spend on this loser.

he's just not that into you if he's married (and other insane variations of being unavailable)

If you're not able to love freely, it's not really love

This is going to be controversial, but I am going to say it anyway. No matter how powerful and real your feelings may be for someone, if that person cannot fully and *honestly* return them and therefore actively love you back, these feelings mean nothing. Sure, they may feel powerful, deep, mythic in scope and proportion. You may "never ever have felt this way before." But who cares? If the person you "love" (notice the snotty quotation marks around that) cannot freely spend his days thinking about you and being with you, *it's not real love*.

The "But His Wife Is Such a Bitch" Excuse

Dear Greg,

I'm dating my married boss. We've kept it on the down-low so no one will find out about it. I really, really love him, and he loves me. I know it's wrong to date a married man, but his wife is *so awful* to him. She calls him names and tells him that he's stupid. They never have sex. He tells me that I'm the only thing keeping him going. How can I leave him when he's going through such a hard time and I love him so much?

Blaire

FROM THE DESK OF GREG

Hey, Down-Low,

Really? We're having this conversation? I'm really going to have to explain to you why you shouldn't be dating a married man? Well, okay: Here is the lowdown on your boss. He's married and having an affair, which indicates to me so many things. First, he's okay with being dishonest. (Nice.) Second, he's fine with cheating on his wife. (Super.) Third, he has no regard for his marriage. (What a gem.) Fourth and most specifically to you, he has no real regard for you, because what you're getting from him is scraps—stolen time that's cloaked in shame. (Just what you always dreamed of as a girl, right?) And because this is a workplace affair, who do you think will be asked to leave when the romance goes sour

> or becomes watercooler fodder that threatens his job and/or marriage? You. And whose reputation as a serious business-person will be compromised? Did you guess you? Good girl. Regardless of how much his marriage sucks or how awful his wife is to him, it obviously isn't that bad or he would get out of it. A good relationship should not be lived in secrecy. Go find yourself one worth living out loud.

I know things seem a lot easier when your affair is with a man whose wife is an evil, shrieking, insulting hag. No matter what their relationship or circumstances are, you are still helping a man cheat on his wife. Let's agree you're better than that.

The "But He's Really a Good Person" Excuse

Dear Greg,

I never thought I'd be in this situation. I know you're not supposed to date married men, but here I am. I met him at a conference out of town, but ended up seeing him for work reasons in the city I live in. We fell in love and one thing led to another. We see each other whenever he's in town, which is often. It would be easy to think all the bad things I should think about this situation, except for the fact that he is a kind, good man. He has never done anything like this before. And he never says anything bad about his wife. We are deeply in love. I'm thirty-six years old and I have never in my life felt anything this powerful before. He says the same thing, too. He talks about leaving his wife, but he has two young

children, and this would be devastating to them. He is
tortured by it all. I feel awful, and yet I also believe
I deserve to feel this kind of love. And if it feels so
huge, it must be real and meant to be. This isn't the
typical dating-a-married-guy story, Greg. This is me. And
it feels completely different.

Belinda

Dear Other Woman,

Hey, smart girl. Good for you to know you deserve to feel
a powerful and profound love. I just think you should have it
with someone who's actually *yours*. There's plenty of guys
out there. Why not get one of your own? Sure, okay, sometimes people fall out of love, marry the wrong person, are
overcome with passion, or make bad choices, all of which can
result in an affair. Here's how you and Ring Finger Fred can
handle this situation now: Stop seeing each other; let him
figure out his life. If he ends up staying with his wife, then
you would have been that girl who was having an affair with
the guy who was never planning on leaving his wife. If he
does leave his wife, then you can start a life with him not
based in shame.

This is no joke, and I'm not even going to try to be glib
(even if I was a little in the letter above). You want love and
you want to be loved and you think you've finally found
it. But he's married. Please try not to ignore that fact. He's

married to someone else. I know you're different, and it's different, but the fact is, he's still married. If there's only one red flag you are unable to ignore in your entire life, please make it this one. There's simply too much at stake for everyone involved.

The "I Should Just Wait It Out" Excuse

Dear Greg,

I started going out with a guy who is really fun and sweet and a breath of fresh air. He calls when he says he's going to, drives sort of far from where he lives to take me out, and we have been having a really nice time together. The only problem is he's going through a really ugly custody battle and he can't stop talking about it. Really. Even when I beg him not to, he can't stop talking about his wife and how much he hates her, what a liar she is, and how he's going to "take her down." I understand this is a difficult time for him, and I don't want to blow this just because it happens to be bad timing. Should I just try to be supportive and listen to him vent about it all?

Pam

FROM THE DESK OF GREG

Dear Midnight at the Oasis,
   Wow. So, he's fun and sweet and a breath of fresh air, but

can't stop spewing bile and talking about his ex-wife. Sounds like a catch. Ladies, I mean it. I'm very sorry that it's so hard to find a decent guy these days, that you'll let any punctual male with the ability to dial the phone and drive a car get away with anything. It's a sad state of affairs and I'm not sure what can be done about it. As for you, it sounds like there's no chance of him being that into you any time soon, if only because there's simply no room for it in his angry little head right now. Here's my vote: It doesn't sound like he's given you good enough reason to keep sitting through his one-man show called "I Want to Kill My Wife." If he misses you, he can get his act together and call you when his head is clearer. In the meantime, you have much better things to do with your time, including going out and buying a ticket to a much higher quality piece of theater.

Again, it's never going to be good news if you have to think of your relationship in terms of "waiting for him." He's not a stock you're supposed to be investing in. He's a man who's supposed to be emotionally available enough to talk to you, see you, and perhaps fall madly in love with you. That's why he's on a date with you. And if you want to ask for the absolute minimum, he can at least have the courtesy to be good company.

IT'S SO SIMPLE

Yes. You are going to meet many men in many different stages of recovering from relationships. If he is really into you, he will get over his issues fast and make sure he doesn't lose you. Or he will make it clear to you how he feels, so there's no mystery, and tell you up front that he's not up to it right now. And then you can best be sure, the minute he is ready, he will run out and find you. *You are not easily forgettable.*

HERE'S WHY THIS ONE IS HARD, by Liz

Because it's you—not someone you read about or heard about or saw on TV. It's you and it's hard. And you deserve happiness just like his wife or his girlfriend does. And sometimes people get married before they've actually met the person they're meant to be with. Or marriages just die and there's nothing left to them. And if they're not married, but somehow deeply distracted by someone else, well, most men are usually coming out of some situation while they get into the next one . . . so why *not* hang on for dear life until he shakes off his ex?

The operative word in both cases here is "wait." *You* have to do the waiting—the biding your time, biting your tongue, keeping your needs quiet. He's so special, that guy. He deserves to have you sit around, putting your life on hold, not getting what you want, while he takes his time sorting it all out. He's that special. You, of course, aren't at all.

Now, I happen to be really good at biding my time and asking for little and being happy with the even less that I get. I haven't personally dated a married man, but I am an expert in dating emotionally unavailable ones. I have to be honest—it feels really noble and romantic and dramatic to be filled with longing and heartache, knowing the man you love, for whatever reason, can't be yours right now. And you're willing to wait for him, because your feelings for him are so very large and profound. (Of course, I am now suspicious that my feelings for them all felt so large and profound precisely *because* they couldn't be mine, but I wouldn't be able to prove that in court.) If you're really comfortable with that, too, and nothing that this book or your friends or your therapist can say will help you change that, then eventually, I hope, like me, you'll eventually just get tired of it.

Sometimes all the psychological help in the world can't do anything. Sometimes boredom just has to set in. You get bored with always having less than what everybody else seems to have, less than what you want. You start thinking that maybe you actually deserve better, not because you learned to love yourself or lost all that weight or saw that great episode on *Dr. Phil*, but just because you got bored. Bored with the same type of misery over and over and over again. That's what happened to me, I think. I hope it will be a lot faster for you.

THIS IS WHAT IT SHOULD LOOK LIKE, by Liz

My friend met a guy who had just broken up with his girlfriend two weeks before, after living with her for three years. She thought that she was just going to be his "rebound" romance. He thought she may be that as well. But even though he could have used the excuse that he wasn't ready yet, because he had "just gotten out of something," he didn't. Because he was really into her, he never let her feel that he wasn't available to her. They are now in a serious relationship.

💡 GREG, I GET IT! By Janine, age 43

I recently met a guy online whose wife had passed away three months earlier. We went out a few times and it was clear he wasn't really ready to be dating. He was deeply grieving and spent a lot of time talking about his wife and how wonderful she was. I was tempted to take care of him, console him, and nurse him through this difficult period. I liked him and had fantasies about what he would be like when he was "better." But then I realized that I didn't want to be with someone who I had to "heal" into the relationship. I told him I didn't feel comfortable dating him so soon after his wife's death, but that I hadn't closed any doors, and would love to see him again when more time had passed. Then I went back online and continued my search.

IF YOU DON'T BELIEVE GREG

A friend of mine was on a first date with a woman who mentioned she was also dating a married man. He immediately told her there wouldn't be a second date, because if she didn't like herself enough to be in a proper relationship, why should he?

What You Should Have Learned in This Chapter

✓ He's married.

✓ Unless he's all yours, he's still hers.

✓ There are cool, loving *single* men in the world. Find one of them to go out with.

✓ If a guy is yelling about his ex-wife or crying over his last girlfriend, try to find someone else to take you to the movies.

✓ He's married.

✓ Don't be that girl.

✓ You are not easily forgotten. Let him find you when he's ready.

Our Super-Good Really Helpful Workbook

List all the things you want or have ever wanted in a man. We'll give you five lines. We'll wait. . . .

1.

2.

3.

4.

5.

Now look at your list. Did "married" or "emotionally unavailable" make that list?

Yeah, we didn't think so. You're far too classy and smart for that.

he's just not that into you if he's a selfish jerk, a bully, or a really big freak

If you really love someone, you want to do things to make that person happy

"He's got so much good in him. He really does. I just wish he wouldn't tell me to shut up all the time." Yeah, that's a problem. Try not to ignore it. I know "he's got so many other great qualities." That's why you fell in love with him in the first place. I know you wouldn't fall in love with an asshole. But here's the trick: Forget about him and his good qualities. Even forget about his bad ones. Forget about all his excuses and what he promises. Ask yourself one question only: Is he making you happy? People are complicated. They are a mixed bag of lovable and dysfunctional qualities. That's why they are so darn confusing. That's why trying to figure them out is a waste of time. Is he making you happy? I don't mean some of the time, on rare occasions, not that often, "but the good still outweighs the bad." Does he make it clear in his actions every day that your happiness is important to him? If the answer is no, cut him loose and go find a man with a higher "good count."

The "He's Really Trying to Be Better" Excuse

Dear Greg,

My boyfriend is selfish. He says he loves me, and he does include me in his life; we are close to each other's families and he is a very good man in many ways. But we have been living together for four years and he never shares household responsibilities, doesn't put any effort into going on nice dates with me, doesn't make a big deal about my birthday, never brings me flowers, won't walk the dog, rarely compliments me, doesn't thank me when I make a nice dinner for him and his friends, isn't that affectionate, and doesn't want to go on nice vacations with me. We talk about it all the time, and he swears that he's trying to change, but his changes are pretty imperceptible.

The question is, can he really love me as much as he says he does, and be this much of a dick?

Paula

Dear A-dick-ded,

You've got to be kidding me. Take your letter, hold it up, and read it to yourself and a friend. If you can't figure out the answer, call the cops, because someone's had their brains stolen.

P.S.: The answer to your question is no. People who are in love with each other generally try to be nice. Some even get a kick out of treating their mate well and trying to make their life better. He may think he loves you, and maybe he does. *But he's really bad at it.* And it's exactly the same result as if he was just not that into you.

Try not to be four years into a relationship when it suddenly dawns on you that the guy you're with is a big, selfish jerk. Chances are Jerk Boy has been trying to show you who he is since day one.

The "It's Just the Way He Was Brought Up" Excuse

Dear Greg,

My boyfriend of a year is perfect in every way. He just happened to grow up in a very dysfunctional family with only one other brother and a crazy mother. I am from a very big, close, loving family. He does not ever want to spend time with my family, and when given the choice, will always stay at home rather than go for a visit. When I do take him with me to family dinners, he's sullen and unfriendly. We talk about it and he says he just isn't into family. It's hard to imagine sharing a future with someone like this, but at the same time, isn't how we get along alone more important? And I think eventually he would get used to my family and come around, don't you? They're really nice people.

Enid

FROM THE DESK OF GREG

Dear All in the Family,

So your boyfriend is perfect in every way except he's not into your family. Wow! That's a pretty big exception. Sure, he's got kind of a good excuse to be selfish. (Because that's all this is about, really.) A lot of people don't list on their "top ten favorite things to do" spending time with other people's family. But aren't you hoping one day to include him in that family? In fact, back in the old days (I don't know exactly when that was, but you know what I mean), your family would have had to approve of *him* before he even got to meet *you*. So don't sell out your family for this dude. If he was really into you, and truly planning on sticking around, he would be doing a little tap dance for your awesome family every time he saw them— and perhaps baking them a little cake as well.

He doesn't have to love your CD collection. He doesn't have to love your shoes. But any good, mature guy better make an attempt to love your friends and family—especially when they're great.

The "It's Not Always Going to Be Like This" Excuse

Dear Greg,

I am dating a guy in medical school. He's overworked, overtired, and gets angry easily. He yells at me when I wake him up by mistake, and he recently screamed at me because he felt I was bothering him when he was in the middle of studying for some big exam. The thing is, I know that this is just temporary, because he's in medical school. He wasn't like this in the beginning when we just started dating and he hadn't started school yet. He was really sweet and thoughtful. And every once in a while he'll feel bad and apologize and tell me how much pressure he's under. I know the real guy is going to come back, Greg.

Denise

P.S.: Besides, I always wanted to marry a doctor!

FROM THE DESK OF GREG

Dear Old Yeller!

I don't care if he's studying to become the next Messiah. There is no reason to yell at anyone ever, unless you are screaming "LOOK OUT FOR THAT BUS!" And it's not temporary. People who yell are people with anger issues who need help. People who yell are people who think they're entitled to yell. Hey, hot stuff, do you want to be that couple? You know—that couple where the guy yells at his wife all the time? Even better, do you want him to be that dad? I didn't think so. Don't wait around for Mr. Hyde to turn back into Dr. Jekyll. Go meet a man who really knows what it means to take care of people.

The "It's Behind Closed Doors That Counts" Excuse

Dear Greg,

I love my boyfriend. We live together and he is really good to me. He takes me on expensive vacations and buys me really lovely, thoughtful presents. I feel very secure with him. My friends are kind of not into him because he happens to make fun of me a little when we're out together. He makes fun of the fact that I didn't go to an Ivy League college, and likes to point out when I say something grammatically incorrect, or when I get a piece of information wrong. He loves to disagree with me in front of other people and make a big deal about me not knowing as much as I should about current affairs. I don't care, I assume it just comes from insecurity. He's not like that when we're alone. I swear. So why should I care? Isn't it how he treats me when we're alone that counts?

Nina

Dear Glutton for Punishment,

He sounds perfect, if you like bad people. Why would you want to be with someone who belittles you so that he can feel superior? And especially in front of your friends! Which Ivy League school has a program in public belittlement? Because that's what this guy majored in if he thinks that insulting you in front of your friends is going to make him seem like anything other than an idiot. And why should you care if he treats you better when you're alone? Because it sounds like he can't wait to get you out in public just so he can humiliate you. Dump Mr. Smarty Pants. And go get a degree in A Man I Can Be Around My Friends With.

The "But He's Just Trying to Help" Excuse

Dear Greg,

I have a boyfriend who really understands what I'm going through. I've always had a weight problem and I've been battling it my whole life. He's a huge gym rat and is very food conscious. He tells me what I can and can't eat. If I want to cheat, he tells me that it will go straight to my fat ass. He lets me know if I'm putting on weight, but he also tells me when I look good and am making progress. I think it's great that he's so understanding of my issue. My friends think he's mean to me. I don't agree. What do you think, Greg?

Nadia

FROM THE DESK OF GREG

Dear Weight Watchers,

This guy doesn't sound like your personal trainer; he sounds like your personal bully. And to remind you, his job title is actually just personal boyfriend. But he's a clever personal bully. He knows that you feel bad about yourself and leaps to take advantage of that. Bullies prey on people weaker than them. Even ones that lift weights every day. It's time you use your quads and hamstrings—to run away from him and never come back.

I'm going to comment on the last three together. There's lots of behavior that can be considered abusive that doesn't include being beaten about the head and neck. That includes getting yelled at, being publicly humiliated, or being made to feel fat and unattractive. It's hard to feel worthy of love when someone is going out of their way to make you feel worthless. Being told to get out of these relationships may not work for you. Knowing that you're better than these relationships is the place to start. You *are* better than these relationships.

The "But Now I'm Playing in the Big Leagues" Excuse

Dear Greg,

I've been on three dates with a guy who's a really great catch. He is a journalist who has an incredibly exciting life—he travels, goes on adventures, and has incredibly interesting observations about it all. He's also really funny. He compliments me and seems to like me and keeps asking me out. He always says he's had a great time with me. But in fact, in the three dates we've had together, he actually hasn't asked me one question about myself. He is obviously really into me, otherwise why would he keep asking me out and telling me how nice I look? Maybe this is what it's like dating exciting guys. He's a great catch, Greg!

Ronda

Dear Captive Audience,

You are so lucky to be with such an exciting guy. You get to watch him perform conversational masturbation on you. Hot. He's clearly as impressed with himself as you are. I hate to tell you this, but he's not into you; he's into how you look listening to him. When I met my wife, all I wanted to do was ask her questions. How else was I going to know what she was all about? Yes, I liked telling her my story too—I wanted to impress her with feats of glory—but it was an even exchange, because I thought *she* was the catch. When two people are connecting, they hunger for information about each other, a sliver of what life is like when you're not together, a glimpse into their past, a peek into their mind, all in hopes of getting under their skin. This guy sounds like a megalomaniac. At the very least he should be asking you what kind of underwear you're wearing.

Remember, you are the catch. They are out to snare you. They are not the tasty little mako that will be so good mesquite grilled in a nice lemon sauce. *You* are. Well, you know what I mean.

The "He's Just Finding Himself" Excuse

Dear Greg,
My boyfriend hasn't had a job in two years. He's really sweet and wonderful, but just doesn't know what he wants to do with his life. He DJs every once and awhile, but basically I support him. (I work and have a little family money.) I know he's really into me—he just needs to figure out what he wants, right? Or maybe he's just depressed?

Julie

FROM THE DESK OF GREG

Dear Bringing Home the Bacon,
So, I don't understand. Do you leave him money on the counter in the morning? Or do you pay him for doing chores around the house? Listen, Moneybags. He may be really into you, but he doesn't seem that into himself, or he wouldn't have let you support him for two years. Therefore, by living off of you, he is behaving in a way that perfectly resembles someone who is just not that into you. A man that's really into you and himself will try to get his act together as fast as

he can. That means, first and foremost, collecting a salary. And just beware: Often these guys, once they do get their lives in order, feel so good about it that now they think they need to go find a new relationship. (After all, no girl of real quality would have put up with the kind of crap he had dished out for so long.) So I say let him go find himself—just not on your dime. Then see if Mr. DJ spins back into your life again.

People go through rough patches all the time. But as the saying goes, when the going gets tough, the tough don't ask to borrow five hundred bucks so they can pay their bar tab down at Paddy's. The only job you need to worry about is the job of finding yourself someone who would never be that comfortable living off of you and your family's money.

The "Maybe It's Just His Little Quirk" Excuse

Dear Greg,

I met a guy who's really sensitive and sweet. The problem is, he doesn't like to be physically affectionate. He tells me that he just doesn't enjoy being touched. We have sex, and it's nice, but he's not that into caressing me, either. Everything else about him is great, so it seems like such a strange complaint. Do you think not wanting to cuddle and be touched is a sign that he's just not that into me? Or could it mean he has intimacy issues? I don't want to dump him over this, but I like physical affection!

Frida

FROM THE DESK OF GREG

Dear Starved for Affection,

Have to say, little suspicious of someone who doesn't like one of the greatest pleasures on earth. What else does he not like that you don't know about yet? Puppies? Babies? Having a soul? And if you like being affectionate for all the obvious reasons, then why would you want to doom yourself to a no-touching zone with Mr. Uncomfortable? Yes, some men have a hard time being physically affectionate, but actually not enjoying it? It's difficult to fathom. He may be really into you, but he's certainly not really compatible with you. I say move on, meet someone who enjoys the things you like, and have a long life filled with playful grab-ass.

You will meet people who don't like to be touched, or kissed, or who don't like sex. You can spend a lot of time trying to fix them, or wondering if you should take it personally. Or you can realize that they simply don't like to do the things you find absolutely essential to your enjoyment of life, and then go find yourself someone who does.

The Rare and Exotic "He's Afraid of the Intimacy of Sleep" Excuse

Dear Greg,

I have been dating a guy for a year who can't sleep in the same bed with me. After we have sex, which is always nice and great, he has to go sleep on the couch. He tells me he just "can't deal." Everything else is fine with our relationship. I just figure he has some intimacy issues that I have to be patient with. Does this have to be a sign that he's just not that into me, or can I just see this through?

Gloria

Dear Freak-Lover,

Here's what I'd like to do: Put money down on the fact that everything is in fact not fine with you and freakboy's relationship. He hasn't slept in the same bed with you for a year? This is a freak who needs to be kicked off your freak-loving couch and shown the bottom of your freak-loving boot. The fact that you even care what this freak thinks of you is just proof that the world has indeed gone mad. Call it curtains on the freak show. Please.

If you date, you will meet your share of weirdos and jerks. That is as sure as death and taxes. The only thing in your control is how long you allow these gentlemen to take up space in your life. In case you're not sure, it should be about ten minutes from when they first display their completely unacceptable behavior (or lizardlike tail). Ten minutes still gives you time to put on all your clothes and make sure you have deleted your number from his cell phone.

IT'S SO SIMPLE

There's a difference between eccentric and insane. "Eccentric" will sometimes wear a velvet jacket. "Insane" will only have sex with you when wearing it. There's a difference between teasing and abuse. Teasing is "Björk called. She wants her dress back." Abuse is "Boy, are you getting *fat*." But the biggest difference is you. You all are ultimately better than the treatment you are receiving from these men.

HERE'S WHY THIS ONE IS HARD, by Liz

I've been implying this in my "Here's Why This One Is Hard" responses, but now I'm just going to come right out with it: There aren't that many good men around. Statistics prove it, articles and books have been written to verify it, and women would be happy to testify under oath about it. And here's another one: There are more good women out there than good men. I bet you've heard or said that one before. Oh, wait, there's this one as well: A lot of men want to date much younger women, so as you get older, there are even fewer men that want to date you. So let's have Greg come over to our house with a little pocket calculator and tell us how, given the pure math of it, we're all going to end up with great men who love us and whom we love back, where there's a passionate mutual attraction, who also treat us like queens.

Exactly. It can't happen. So yes, it seems logical, reasonable, and down right savvy for all the fantastic, smart, healthy, funny, kind women out there to start thinking about lowering their expectations. Because I don't know about you, but I hate being single. I hate going to parties alone. I hate sleeping alone. I hate waking up alone. I hate knowing that every single boring errand I have to do, I'm going to do alone. I hate not having sex. I hate cooking for one and shopping for one. I hate going to weddings. I hate people asking me why I'm still single. I hate people not asking me why I'm still single. I hate my birthday because I'm still single. I hate having to think about possibly becoming a single mother because I'm single. Have I made myself clear?

Obviously I don't think people should go out with someone who is abusive to them. But there are subtle degrees of abuse. There are many shades of Mr. Wrong. And these guys that we're talking about? They're not *just* assholes. They can be nice sometimes, too. And there are many days when I personally think it's better to be with someone who your friends might hate but will help you carry in the groceries, than be alone. So I said it. This one is very hard for me. It's so hard for me that I think Greg has to take over. It's too difficult. I am deeply pragmatic, so given the sheer statistics, I don't have a clue on what to say. I know we have to love ourselves and think we deserve happiness and be optimistic. I also think it sucks to be single. Greg, are you really telling us that we should just stay single and picky and not settle (and thus not settle down) until we have met the person we think is the one? It's really lonely out there. You take this one. I don't have a clue.

GREG RESPONDS:

We are now at the crux of the whole matter, aren't we? It's not so funny when we really get to the painful, lonely center of it all. I get that it is a much more profound problem than he's just not that into you. I have sat up many nights with so many friends (and my sister) in tears trying to get them to believe that they are better than the men who are messing up their lives. So I will try to answer this as best I can.

Being lonely, being alone, for many people, sucks. I get it, I get it, I get it. But still I have to say that, yes, my true belief is that being with somebody who makes you feel shitty or doesn't honor the person you are, is worse.

The statistics are bleak. But don't use statistics to keep you down or keep you frightened. You can't do anything with these statistics except scare yourself and your girlfriends. So I say, "Fuck statistics." It's your life—how dare you not have faith in it! The only story that has ever helped me, Greg Behrendt, live my life successfully is the story of faith; I believe that life will turn out well. More fervently, I believe that you have no other choice than to believe that. I am writing this book, and women will be reading it, because we are all tired of operating from a place of fear. You want to believe that you are better than all the crap you've been taking from all these men all these years. Well you are. You are an excellent, foxy human being worthy of love, and the only way you can pursue that idea is by honoring yourself. At the very least this means ridding your world of dudes who are not worthy and setting a standard of excellence in your daily life.

Let's start with this statistic: You are delicious. Be brave, my sweet. I know you can get lonely. I know you can crave companionship and sex and love so badly that it physically hurts. But I truly believe that the only way you can find out that there's something better out there is to first *believe* there's something better out there. I'll believe it for you until you're ready.

THIS IS WHAT IT SHOULD LOOK LIKE, by Greg 👤

My friend Amy is deathly afraid of clowns, so her husband Russell makes sure she never sees one or is near one. Now this might not seem like a difficult task or one that requires great personal sacrifice, until you've actually tried to avoid all the clowns in the world. Oh, it's not as easy as you'd think. You'd be amazed at how many clowns are out there. But Russell does it because after ten years of marriage, he still wants to protect his wife from things that frighten her.

GREG, I GET IT! By Georgia, age 33

I went out with this guy who really was not nice to my friends. He would barely smile or make eye contact with them when he'd meet them. And if he got into a conversation with them, he wouldn't ask them any questions about themselves. Sometimes when they would be talking to him, he would turn away from them mid-sentence. He wouldn't say he didn't like them, but that's just the way he was. Okay, so I'll admit it. I didn't break up with him over it. He ended up dumping me. But now looking back, I'm glad I'm not with someone like that. I want to be with someone who is charming and loves my friends. I want to someday go out with someone who my friends meet and call me the next day and say "Oh my God, he's *great!*"

IF YOU DON'T BELIEVE GREG

A guy friend of mine refuses to break up with a woman he's engaged to because he's scared. (Yes, we're a classy species.) When I beg the guy to pull the plug, he always says the same thing: "Greg, I'm waiting for the big fight. I'm just waiting for the big fight." In the meantime, he picks on, bickers with, needles his fiancée, just so he can have the "big fight" and get it over with. It's not pretty, but I hope it scares you just a bit.

100% of the guys polled said they have never tried to torture or humiliate a girl they were really into. Well, that's a start.

What You Should Have Learned in This Chapter

✓ Life is hard enough as it is without choosing someone difficult to share it with.

✓ You deserve to be with someone who is nice to you all the time. (You have to be nice to them, too.)

✓ There's never a reason to shout at someone unless they are in imminent danger.

✓ Freaks should remain at the circus, not in your apartment.

✓ You already have one asshole. You don't need another.

✓ Make a space in your life for the glorious things you deserve.

✓ Have faith. What other choice is there?

Our Super-Good Really Helpful Workbook

If you're in a relationship that you suspect is not good for you, but you're not sure, do this simple exercise:

Take out a tape recorder. Tell the story of your relationship into it. Play it out loud. Imagine that your best friend in the whole world is telling you the story instead of you. Would you want better for her?

If it's impossible for you to think you deserve better, try to at least believe one of your friends who thinks you deserve better . . . just long enough to get you out of the relationship.

don't listen to these stories

Sure. There are the stories. Guys that get pursued by some girl first and she ends up being the love of his life; the guy that treats this girl that he sometimes sleeps with like shit for a couple of years, but she keeps at him and now he's a devoted husband and father; the guy who doesn't call a girl that he's slept with for a month, and then calls her and they live happily ever after; the woman who is sleeping with the married guy who she ends up marrying and having a blissful long-term marriage with.

We don't want you to listen to these stories. **These stories don't help you. These stories are the exceptions to the rule. We want you to think of yourself as the rule. Thinking of yourself as the exception is what got you into this mess in the first place. Tell your friends to stop telling you these stories. Whenever you hear one of these stories, a story where some woman was treated badly but it all worked out okay in the end, just put your hands up to your ears and go "la-la-la-la-la!"**

You are exceptional, but not the exception!!

now what do you do?

Okay. We just laid waste to your personal lives. We admit it. If all the women in this book listened to these answers, there would right now be a fresh crop of newly single women out there. Therefore, it seems like it's our duty to discuss what one must do *after* the breakup.

We're not psychiatrists or very girly (particularly Liz), so we're not going to talk about candles and bubble baths and sending yourself flowers. But I think we could ask you to at least try to notice, even just a tiny bit, how good it feels to be out of a relationship with someone who actually wasn't that into you. Can you at least feel that sense of relief? When you think about it, making all those excuses for someone and trying to "figure someone out" takes up a lot of energy. Think of all the time you've opened up for so many other more positive things besides obsessing over *him*. Yes, breakups are painful, even from someone you may have only dated a few times. You may have been really excited about him and had a lot of hopes for the future. But how empowering to have the mental clarity to say, "He just wasn't that into me." Can you imagine that girl in the future? Nothing will be able to stop her!

Now, there's a million things you can do after a breakup; what you do during that time—yoga, affirmation tapes, murder—is your business. But basically you're going to have to feel the pain, you're going to have to go through it, and then you're going to have to get over it. All we can try to do in this book is help you do it differently in the future. The first thing we're going to recommend is setting some standards.

Reset Your Standards

Sure, you say, "But I have standards." Well, your standards led you to this book, so let's raise them. Let's set a dignified bar for you to exist at. Let's put you in charge of how it's going to go next time. (But you ask, "What if there isn't going to be a next time?" And we say, "Stow that bad-news cargo on the sure-to-sink ship. Because that ship is about to hit Sad Island and we don't want you on it.")

A standard is setting a level for yourself of what you will or won't tolerate. You get to decide how it's going to be for you. You can now design the person you want to be in the future, and the standards you want to have. Write your new standards down so you'll never ever forget them, no matter how cute he is or how long it's been since you've had sex. (Okay, we admit it, some of our workbook things were a little silly, but this one we mean.) Make sure you know what you stand for and what you believe in.

And because we obviously think we know better than you

(we got a book deal, didn't we?), we're going to give you some standard suggestions.

STANDARD SUGGESTIONS

I will not go out with a man who hasn't asked me out first.

I will not go out with a man who keeps me waiting by the phone.

I will not date a man who isn't sure he wants to date me.

I will not date a man who makes me feel sexually undesirable.

I will not date a man who drinks or does drugs to an extent that makes me uncomfortable.

I will not be with a man who's afraid to talk about our future.

I will not, under any circumstances, spend my precious time with a man who has already rejected me.

I will not date a man who is married.

I will not be with a man who is not clearly a good, kind, loving person.

Now it's your turn. Only you know the standards you haven't set for yourself. Write them down. Don't forget them.

MY SUPER-HELPFUL STANDARDS THAT I WILL NEVER EVER FORGET OR FORSAKE NO MATTER HOW HOT I THINK HE IS:

1.

2.

3.

4.

5.

6.

7.

8.

9.

10.

Glossary

Now that you've set your standards, we want to make sure you keep them. People talk about looking out for the red flags, but they don't often tell you how to find them. That's why we've comprised a handy glossary of the most-often-used words that guys say when what they really mean is "I'm just not that into you."

SEEMINGLY INNOCENT WORDS AND PHRASES THAT CAN ALSO BE USED FOR EVIL

	What it should mean:	What it sometimes means:
Friend	I would never do anything to intentionally hurt you.	I'm just not that into you.
Busy	I was just inaugurated president of the United States today.	I'm just not that into you.
Bad Boy	A guy you should stay away from.	A guy you should stay away from.
I'm not ready	I can't find my pants.	I'm just not that into you.
Call me	I just dropped my cell phone in the ocean and I lost your number.	I'm just not that into you.
Not into family	I don't want to date your mom.	I'm just not that into you.
Fear of intimacy	A fear of being intimate.	I'm just not that into you.

14

q&a with greg

I know some of these ideas are new to people and hard to digest. Because of that, I feel Greg still has a little explaining to do, to make sure no one walks away with the wrong idea. Okay, I'm not going to lie—I can use Greg to explain a few things . . . to me. Some of these ideas are hard to digest.

—Liz

1) **Greg, seriously, are you really sure I can't ask the guy out? Guys say I'm intimidating. I should be allowed to help them out a bit.**

Most of the great things we want in life are intimidating. That's what makes life so darn exciting. Do you really have time for a guy who's so afraid of you that he's not even capable of inviting you for coffee?

2) **Greg, are you so sure there are so many great guys out there, that I can just throw all these other less-than-perfect guys away?**

I don't know how to answer that except to say that being in a good relationship is much better than being in a bad relationship, and you'll never be able to be in a good relationship if you're sticking with Mr. Shitty What's His Name. Only you can know if the relationship you're in isn't good enough for you. A good indication that it's not is if you're only staying with What's His Name because you're scared.

3) What if I would rather be with someone who might not be that into me than be alone?

I get it. You can feel like crap and be alone. Or feel like crap and at least have someone to spend the holidays with. Got it. It seems like it might be a fair trade, except for the fact that it means the only two options you are giving yourself involve feeling like crap. By staying with the guy who's not that into you, you are ensuring that you're never going to find one that is. I say, not to anyone's surprise, take the risk of not having someone to spend Christmas with, possibly feel lonely for a while, but know that you're doing it for a much bigger payoff at the end.

4) Greg, do you really think there are that many men out there who are capable of being as loving as you think I deserve?

Yes. I do. I do. I do. Otherwise I wouldn't be writing this book.

5) Greg, in the book you say that I shouldn't talk to my ex-boyfriend unless he's begging to get back together

with me. But then you also say that I should be suspicious of a guy that wants to get back together with me after he's broken up with me. What's up?

Well, my first point was, I want you to see the difference between an ex who just misses you and needs a fix, and a man who realizes he made a mistake and seriously wants to get back together with you. But even then, I think you must proceed with caution and truly question this man's motives. And I definitely want you to stay away from any man that keeps breaking up with you on a regular basis.

6) **Do you think a bad guy can change into a good guy, within a relationship?**

I'm loath to say this to someone who might be coming from an unhappy situation and is wanting me to validate it. I believe that anything is possible. However, my experience has been that most men do not change, and the ones I've seen change only changed when they met new women.

7) **What if I only seem to be attracted to guys who are just not that into me?**

Okay, so you have this crazy quirk that somehow makes you able to sniff out the men that are going to end up being emotionally unavailable to you. We can talk about why that is and what your priorities are that make these men seem attractive to you. However, what we can most quickly rectify is how long you stick around once you know that he's just not that into you. A lot of guys, good and bad, are going to fly in your direction. Which ones you pick to invest your time in is where you have your control. Immediately.

8) **C'mon, Greg. Admit it. Sometimes there are real, sincere reasons why a guy who really likes me isn't able to get in a serious relationship with me. It doesn't have to mean he's just not that into me.**

Maybe there are men like that out there, maybe there aren't. This is the only thing you need to remember: Mr. I'm Just Not Up For It is exactly the same guy as Mr. I'm Just Not That Into You. Both guys don't want to be with you. One of them may say he can't be with you, but it's still the same result. He isn't going to be with you. Don't let his personal complications confuse you into waiting around for him. He's not able to be really into you. And you deserve better.

9) **You seem to have a fascination with seeing women in their underwear. What's that all about?**

I don't think there's anything sexier than a woman in her underwear. Sue me!

closing remarks from greg

Don't waste the pretty

I was talking to a girl I had just met in Austin, Texas, one night, who was having a very common "He's just not that into you" problem. She had met a guy at work who right away came on hot and heavy. They had sex on the first date, and then he disappeared. Figuratively, that is. He didn't go anywhere and they still saw each other, but the guy she met was gone. He was replaced by a guy who wouldn't make eye contact, was grumpy and tired all the time, didn't really want to have sex with her unless he was drunk, and never made formal plans to see her. Oh, and he told her that she was the greatest girl he'd ever met, that he'd never felt this way before, and (you guessed it) that he was scared. I wanted to meet him so I could put him in a glass case and tour him around the world with a sign that reads THIS IS THE GUY WE'VE BEEN WARNING YOU ABOUT. STEP AWAY FROM THE GLASS! I was very excited to reveal the newly minted "He's just not that into you" concept. "She's going to be blown away like the girls at *Sex and the City* were and on her way to a new and happier reality," was my thought. However, as I was sharing my wisdom, I could sense some tension.

"How do you know I'll find someone else?" she asked.

"I don't. I just don't see the point in being in a relationship that appears to be damaging and beneath you. You are a really cool, obviously very cute . . ."

"You don't know me!" she practically shouted, cutting me off mid-sentence. "How do you know I can do better? You've only just met me. And why do you care anyway?"

Wow! She had me dead to rights. I was stunned for a moment but then I remembered why I'm doing this, and I said to her what I would say to you now. "I don't need to know you to know that at the very least you ought to think that way about yourself." And why do I care? Or better yet, who am I to be giving advice to others? I am a formerly single guy who gave those same lame excuses, so I know what these guys are really doing. When I met my wife, Amiira, I became a different guy, a man who showed up, suited up, and was glad to do so, because I believe in love the verb, not the noun. I believe in letting the woman I love know I love her all the time with my actions. Why do I care about you? Because I have a sister and many women friends whom I love dearly, despite their unwillingness to hear the clanging bells of a crappy relationship. Because I have a *wonderful* sister and so many *amazing* women friends who still don't have the confidence to believe that they deserve better and will only find someone better after they unload the dead weight of an inadequate suitor. Because I have an *incredible* sister and so many *brilliant* women friends who don't yet truly accept that profound love is uplifting, joyous, inspiring, and intoxicating, and that they should never settle for anything less. Shitty relationships make you feel shitty, and that's not what you were put on this earth for.

It's all fun and games to have some insight and a witty reply to your letters, but at the core the "He's just not that into you" concept can truly have a magical transcendent effect. It's not bad news if it helps you free yourself from a relationship that is beneath you. And we both know that only you can free yourself. I don't pretend to know how to fix you. I do know how to help you recognize the problem. I do know that you are worthy of having great relationships and an even better life. I do think you are beautiful and somewhere deep down inside you know it too, otherwise you wouldn't be here. I believe life is a speedy and awesome gift, so don't waste the pretty. If you are reading this, *you* want something better. If you are reading this, I want something better for you too.

—Greg

closing remarks from liz

Greg can be really annoying

Greg can be really annoying. I understand. I work with him.
Even during the writing of this book he has managed to dash
my hopes and dreams about men I have been optimistic
about dating. It seems no one is good enough for Greg. It's
impossible to please Greg, with his high demands on men's
behavior. Who does Greg think he is? So what if my guy calls
me on Monday instead of on the weekend like he said he
would? What's so wrong with that, Greg? Jeez. It's one lousy
day. With your impossibly high standards, Greg, I'm going to
be dating, like, every eight years.

He's also so absolute. He really doesn't live in the gray
area. I do. In fact, I bought a co-op and moved into the gray
area. It's the right choice for me (even though the mainte-
nance is really high). I don't know theoretically what I'd do if
my spouse whom I was married to for fifteen years and had
three kids with cheated on me. Greg does. He's absolute.

Also, I'm a pessimist, and Greg's unswerving optimism is really irritating. It annoys me when he tells me that he believes everyone—if they truly believe it and are open to it—will find a good person to love. I don't believe that's true. I think some of those people who are single and ready to have love in their lives are going to get cancer and die, or get hit by a car, or just never find love with a good man and maybe just settle. (That's why I'm not the one answering all the questions!)

I also know that I get really lonely. And Greg has been with his wife for over five years now. He doesn't know from single person's lonely. Easy for him to sit at the lazy Susan of love, and tell me to keep turning until I find just the right dish. He's got a date for every Valentine's Day for the rest of his damn life.

But I do think he's right—a lot of the time—which is the most annoying part of it all. Greg is the older brother we all should have in our lives (and in our heads). He demands that men treat us better than even we think they should. We have been conditioned to expect so little, told not to be demanding, not to seem needy. But what would happen if all the women in the world listened to Greg—if we all started insisting that men keep true to their word, treat us with respect, shower us with the appropriate amount of love and affection? I think there would be an awful lot of better-behaved men in the world. That's all I'm saying.

And in terms of Greg's outlook on the world, well, I can give you incredibly valid arguments, backed up with statistics, flow charts, and diagrams, for why my pessimism is the more realistic outlook to have. But will it make me any happier?

That's where I'm at now, at forty-one and still single. What are the points of view and attitudes that are going to make me a happier person? I'm already smart enough. I need a constant dose of happy now.

If you are reading this book, chances are you are someone who has spent too much time with men who have given you too little—meaning, you could use a little Greg voice in your head. What woman, really, couldn't use a man in her ear, reminding her that she's smart and valuable and worthy and gorgeous and deserving of everything she ever wanted? Not a one. The world out there feeds us a lot of messages telling us otherwise. I think Greg's yelling at us so loud in the hope that he can drown out some of that other noise.

I hope this book was helpful to you. I hope it made you a laugh a little, in recognition. And I hope you find fantastic, healthy, life-changing love, just the way you had imagined it.

With perhaps a few surprises thrown in just for fun.

—Liz

17

life after *he's just not that into you*

From Liz

There's nothing like cowriting a book called *He's Just Not That Into You* to make you relive every mistake you've ever made in your love life and reminisce about all the wonderful men who have ever rejected you. *Let me tell you—it was really fun.* I came to realize that I *literally* had made every mistake in the book. I also understood that the reason I was the one who suggested writing this book to Greg was because I was the one who needed to read it the most. (I think I figured that out when I saw the look of outright horror and pity on Greg's face as I was telling him my approximately twentieth horrible dating story. *Good times.*) But the great news is, while writing the book I experienced all the things that many women who have read the book told us they went through—the epiphanies, the empowerment, and the resolve that I was never going to make those mistakes again. It *did* change the way I dated, thought about men, and handled my relationships. This book, in many ways, changed my life. So, in case you didn't already know and at the risk of sounding completely horrid—I am not just the coauthor of this book. I'm its number one fan.

But when Greg and I were asked if there was anything more we wanted to add to this book, I knew that I did have something I wanted to get off my chest. As someone who took this book very much to heart and yet is still out there dating, I felt that I wanted to discuss "life after *He's Just Not That Into You*." I started to experience a whole *process* after writing this book and implementing its basic philosophy into my life. I realized there were stages to this process, and they were very distinct. I also heard and saw that other women were going through them as well. They may not have gone through the stages in the order that I did, or experienced all of them as I have, but I have heard similar enough stories that I felt inclined to write the stages down in an order that makes sense to me.

If you have just read this book for the first time or read the book but didn't care for it so much, I am inclined to tell you to read no further. This section really is for the women who are fans of the book, who used it to make great changes in their lives—and who are still out there dating. It is a chapter that can come only with perspective—and I don't want you to get ahead of yourself. For that reason, if you have just read *He's Just Not That Into You* for the first time, I suggest putting this section down and reading it in a year or two—and only if you feel like you need a little extra encouragement.

So here we go: the stages of Life After *He's Just Not That Into You*, according to Liz.

Exaltation
(Otherwise known as "He's out of my phone, and he's out of my life!")

The first thing that often happens after reading our book is the realization that we're geniuses and we've changed your life. Okay, maybe not. Maybe it doesn't happen that quickly. (And maybe you don't think we're actual *geniuses*.) There might be some resistance at first. Maybe you're still holding on to a relationship or a crush that you aren't willing to give up on yet. For some, there can be a slight depression, looking back and thinking about how much time you may have wasted. (Trust me, I understand.) But, for many, eventually Greg's nagging, aggressive, slightly annoying-at-times voice finally gets through. You are unable to ignore it any longer. You get out of the dead-end relationship. You realize the crush isn't going anywhere. You stop texting that guy. And lo and behold, pretty soon you feel better. And not just like "Wow, I feel so much better." I mean better like when someone who has been punching you in the face for three hours finally stops—like *ecstatically better*. You feel lighter, so light in fact that you are floating. The dark cloud has lifted off of you, and you can now achieve anything because you are, in fact, a superfox. Because you refuse to waste the pretty. You are powerful, sexy, and beautiful and will not take any shit anymore. The world has now changed. It is not the sad, dark place where at every turn of a corner there was that guy who was making you feel small. The world is filled with love and hope and possibility because all your thoughts and time and energy have now been freed. You are elated and ready to soar.

You may even have a nice bout of beginner's luck. When I had just finished writing the book, but it had not come out yet, and I was fully indoctrinated into the *He's Just Not That Into You* mindset, I went to a party. There was a guy there who flirted with me. Everyone around us was giggling about how it looked like we had hit it off so well. At the end of the flirty night, he gave me his website address and told me to have a look at these photographs he had taken and "e-mail me and tell me what you think." He left, and everyone I knew swarmed around me to find out what had happened. I told them, and the only person who didn't think it was completely exciting that this man gave me his website address was me—the girl with Greg's pesky, sarcastic voice in her head saying, *"A website address? He gave you his lousy website address? Wow, that's lame."*

Lo and behold, the very next day he called me. Somehow website guy had miraculously figured out that he could get my number from our mutual friend, pick up a phone, call me, and ask me out! Now, that particular gentleman didn't ultimately work out, but at the time it felt like the great big Dating Gods were trying to send me a message that I was on the right track.

So, step one: You see the light. You feel better. You realize we are the smartest people ever to have walked the planet. You may consider nominating us for a Nobel Prize. (We thank you for that sentiment but feel it is perhaps overestimating our contribution to the course of world events at this time.) Greg and I are really glad we helped you feel better and make really positive changes in your life.

Loneliness
(Otherwise known as "Great, what the hell do I do now?")

So. You made some changes. You broke up with the boyfriend who just can't get over his ex. You stopped seeing the guy who "just isn't good at relationships." You stopped e-mailing the guy with whom you had one date three weeks ago but who keeps writing that you two "definitely have to hang out again." More important, you cleared out of your mind all of those excuses that you once made for men, all the ones that seemed so right at the time and now make you shake your head and think, *I can't believe I tried to convince myself of that!* Instead, all you are left with now is the understanding of what it's really supposed to look like. You have the space to think about the great relationship you will most certainly find. Your imagination is now free to think about that guy who will most definitely appear now that you are so brave and strong. You start thinking about true love again, about what that looks like, feels like. You remember how much you want it and how you had forgotten that it was even a possibility.

And then it hits you. If you have deleted all those addresses from your cell phone, if you have raised your standards so that you have eliminated the entire demographic of game-playing, noncommittal, selfish, freakish, emotionally unavailable, completely ambivalent about you men from your list of potential suitors—who the hell is there left to date?

When we did *The Oprah Winfrey Show* there was one woman on the program who really took our advice to heart. She ended up breaking up with her no-good boyfriend. When we went back on the show I asked the producer how this woman was doing. The producer shrugged and said, "Well, to be honest—*she's really lonely.*" I understood immediately what she meant. For me, the jubilation of finally realizing what I'm worth and what I'm not going to put up with anymore slowly, eventually moved on to utter, bone-crushing loneliness. Well, aren't I so noble, going to another wedding on my own? How fantastic it is not to settle and to get to carry my groceries home all by myself. Well, good for me, I get to spend Valentine's Day with my mother (not that she didn't appreciate it).

I don't know about you, but I wanted my reward. A huge, seismic shift had occurred in my entire outlook on love and dating, and I believed the heavens should honor me by delivering to me a really nice boyfriend. Unfortunately, life doesn't work like that. Sometimes it does, and those are the stories that give you hope (and sometimes make you want to jump out the window, if I am being truly honest). But most often, the reward for feeling better about yourself and no longer letting people treat you poorly is just that—feeling better about yourself and not having people treat you poorly.

But, I have to say, there is something else that comes in to fill the vacuum that our book creates. It may seem like a consolation prize, but ultimately it's everything. Replacing the mediocre relationships, halfhearted men, and meaningless e-mails and texts is not just bone-crushing loneliness. It's *confidence*. It is the miraculous emotion that rolls in to replace all the relationship rubble that has been swept away. No one is making you feel like you aren't enough. No situation is making you feel unlovable. There is just you. There is just you and your standards, and soon enough there is confidence. And the more of it that comes, the more positive reinforcement you will get from the outside world. And then, the more it continues to grow. No, it's not a handsome man whisking you off your feet, but it's the thing that will get you there more assuredly than anything else. It's confidence. And you must not underestimate the power and gift of that.

Temptation
(Otherwise known as "The devil comes in many disguises.")

TEMPTATION #1
The One Who Didn't Get Away

At the height of the book's popularity a guy asked me out. He took me to dinner. He was flirtatious and said he would call me, which he did. I called him back. He never called me back. I saw him at a party, where he sat down right next to me and started paying a lot of attention to me. He said he would call me. He did but never asked me out. I was astounded. Are you kidding me? You're going to do that to *me*? Don't you know I literally wrote the book on the subject? But more than being astounded—I was amused. Because I was now a superhero, imbued with superhuman powers of detecting mixed messages, of immediately defending myself against men who really were just not that into me, no matter what clever disguises they used. I threw my head back and laughed: "Oh, how I might have fallen for his little tricks in the past! But not now! They are useless against my *He's Just Not That Into You* superpowers!" I smiled, thinking about what I would have possibly

172

thought in the past about his behavior: "Maybe he was too busy to call, and seeing me at that party reminded him of how much he liked me." Or, "Maybe he can't make a date because he doesn't know what his work schedule is yet, but he's calling so obviously he must like me!" Ah, how strong I am now; how protected I am from these feeble attempts to weaken me!

But just as Superman had his kryptonite, you will meet a man (I would say you can count on it) who will have two very important things going for him. First and foremost, you will really, really, really like him. And second, he will have a really, really, *really* good excuse. It's almost like what happens when an incredibly powerful vaccine is found to conquer a disease—the disease then learns how to mutate into something stronger and more powerful in order to survive. So it is with this man—he will have a powerful strain of an excuse. It will probably have something to do with a child, a recent divorce, or a really huge project at work. And you will allow yourself to fall for it, which, in a sense, you should, as life happens and nothing is truly black-and-white and sometimes you simply need more information in order to make an intelligent decision. But you let it go on too long. Much longer than you know you should. Because you really, really like him. And he seemed to have a really good excuse, such a good excuse that it may take weeks or months to wrap your brain around the sad, disappointing truth. Really? Those damn six words again? He found a way to pierce through your armor, zap you of your superhero strength, send a virus through your hard drive—whatever metaphor you want to use—and you were rendered temporarily powerless. You can't believe it's true—it just can't be—no, really? You realize he's just not that into you. Oh, for Pete's sake.

You thought it could never happen again. And here you are. It's really depressing.

And now you're not just despondent over another romantic disappointment. You are furious with yourself that you let it happen again. But you know better now! How could this have happened?

Well, I'll tell you how it happened. Love is a drug. I know, not the most original of concepts, but it's true. And sometimes no matter how rehabilitated you are, the drug gets you. Particularly if it's been a long time since you've used the drug—then it really can take hold. Love is something most of us want very badly in our lives, sometimes more than we even want to admit. And when we get close to getting it, when we are reminded of how great it feels to have it, even if it's for a moment, even if it's just a whiff of it, we may forget everything we believe in. Don't beat yourself up about it. We understand. And the unbelievable, fantastic, let's organize a parade to celebrate the news of it all is, you will never ever let it go on as long as you would have in the past. Once you have read *He's Just Not That Into You*, no matter how you may slip up, no matter how many steps you may take backward—you can't go too far astray. The *He's Just Not That Into You* bell cannot be unrung. Thank God for that.

TEMPTATION #2
I Can Do This

Then there's just complete and utter desperation. You are lonely. You are horny. You think no one will ever love you again. So you keep calling that guy who's only making the mildest attempt at keeping a connection with you. You suggest hanging out together. You have sex with him. You have sex with him again. You keep sleeping with him—always at your suggestion. You text him dirty little notes. You two are now "hanging out." You know, deep down, that he's just not that into you, that you are powering the entire nonrelationship. But it's all right, because now, because of the book, *you know he's just not that into you, which is different. It's okay to go out with someone who's just not that into you, as long as you are clear about the fact that he's just not that into you, right?* Then you're not deluding yourself. You don't have false hope. It's like you've learned the rules of the game and now you're using them to your advantage. And besides, IT'S BEEN A REALLY LONG TIME SINCE YOU'VE HAD A DATE, SO BACK OFF! Oh, I know. We can be very clever with the mind games we play on ourselves.

I tried that philosophy. I thought that somehow if I knew his oh-so-complicated "situation" was just a smoke screen for the fact that he would never want to be in a relationship with me, then he couldn't really hurt my feelings. Because *I knew.* But it's so funny. A guy taking two days to call you back, or two weeks to want to see you again when you're sleeping with him, still hurts your feelings no matter how clever you think you're being. (Unless you really don't like him—then that's a different story.)

The good news is, just as you are able to identify a lame excuse without equivocation, you are also able to recognize immediately what that sick feeling in the pit of your stomach is: Pain. Longing. Hurt feelings. And these feelings are now even more unpleasant to experience because you have been living without them for so long. So you know, more quickly than ever, that it's absolutely unacceptable to let anyone make you feel like that. I don't think we will ever truly be able to escape Greg's irritating voice in our heads, and that's not a bad thing at all.

So, yes, I can tell you with utmost assuredness that there will be some temptations, and you may slide back a little. There have been a few instances since we wrote *He's Just Not That Into You* when I have completely reverted back to my old self, when I have turned back into that really captivating girl who regales her friends with a mesmerizing story like "Well, he called me on Tuesday, but he didn't ask me out, so I didn't know if I should call him back, so I waited until Wednesday, and then I e-mailed him—but then he didn't e-mail me back until Friday, and I don't know if that's because he was mad that I didn't call him back or . . ."

I felt ridiculous.

Because it just feels too bad to be that girl. Once you start treating yourself with more respect and feeling like the strong, confident woman you are, it just simply becomes too appalling to stay in a situation where some guy is hurting your feelings on a regular basis. Once you start going long stretches filled with well-being and self-esteem, your ability to stand emotional pain becomes very weak—and again, that's the really good news.

Balance
(Otherwise known as "Settling in for the long haul.")

A few years ago I got really into eating a low-carb diet. Who didn't? Goodness knows, no good is going to come from a bowl of pasta. And bread? I would shun it at restaurants, waving my hand at the basket, asking them to please take away that devil food. And I lost weight. And I felt better. Because, really, a muffin is just a toned-down cupcake and don't let anyone tell you differently. And then a couple months go by, or a year, and I started thinking—what the hell is wrong with eating a nice piece of bread every once in a while? Isn't it considered the staff of life? And you know what else? Eating a delicious bowl of spaghetti carbonara isn't going to kill me. People have been doing it in Italy for years, thank you very much. Okay, some appear a little portly, but you know what? They all seem really *happy*.

My point being: Sometimes you just get sick and tired of being on a diet, or even of just thinking a particular way. One day recently I met up with a friend I hadn't seen in a long time. She sat down and said immediately, "Oh my God, I'm so mad at *He's Just Not That Into You* right now." I immediately laughed and exclaimed, "Oh my God, me too!" She continued. "Why *can't* I go to his building and leave a box of Mallomars with his doorman if I feel like it? He told me he loves Mallomars, and I love Mallomars too, and I happened to see them at the supermarket. So what if I just went out with him once!" I screamed back, "I know—the guy I'm dating really *is* getting over a difficult breakup! Why *do* I have to be so suspicious about that?" She said she hated Greg right now. I said I did too. We were tired. We were tired of having to be so *conscious*, of having to be on guard. We were tired of having to be so goddamn vigilant with our love lives and our standards. We were tired of Greg's voice in our ears every time a man even started to flirt with us. We were sick and tired of this new diet we were on, and we wanted to break it. And we did. She left the guy the Mallomars and asked him out for their second date. I kept hanging on in vain to the idea that this guy was going to stop talking about his ex-girlfriend and realize he was ready to love me.

I'm not sure what happened with the Mallomars guy, but I do know that I eventually ended it with my guy. But I wasn't regretful that I got emotionally involved in the situation. You have to give things a shot. And you know what? If you want to leave a box of Mallomars for some guy, who's to tell you not to? Ask the guy out if you feel like it. We can't stop you. At the end of the day, it's your life, and it's your judgment. You may have a long journey ahead of you before you meet your guy. (Hopefully you don't, but just in case . . .) You may be confronted by a lot of confusing situations along the way. You'll be at different stages of self-esteem versus loneliness when you are confronted with them, and that might alter how you respond to them. But, ultimately, you're going to have to make these judgment calls all on your own. Sometimes you will make decisions that empower you and honor you, and sometimes you're going to cheat and maybe go against your better instincts for a bit—just at the off chance that this is one of the exceptions to the rule.

If you're like me, and you have taken this book's positive, empowering message to heart and you were not rewarded with the love of your life ringing your doorbell and changing the course of your life forever, then you might want to go easy on yourself. Life, love, dating—it's all a process. There will be highs and lows, disappointments and temptations, and it all might take awhile. If you are just so lonely that you simply have to get into a less than ideal situation, for God's sake, get out of it before the guy makes you cry or mope in bed all day. (But please, don't ever date a married man, no matter how lonely you feel. Can we all agree on that?) The minute you start feeling those familiar pangs of sadness and longing and obsessing, please pull the plug. If you take nothing else away from this book, please remember that nothing is worse than longing for someone who doesn't want you. Even loneliness is better, because with loneliness you at least have hope and possibility and imagination. But being in a situation where you start to feel hurt and small and rejected, even though it may be a nice little break from the tedium of no dates and no stories to tell your friends, will rob you of your newfound confidence and self-esteem. And nothing is really worth that.

You may want to forget that for a little bit. We understand. And we'll let you, because life is unfair, the world is an imperfect place, and we are all just trying our best. But please, eventually, come back to us. You are worth it. No matter how long you end up being without a relationship, you will always be worth it. You've worked too hard and come too far to sell yourself down the river for some guy who makes you laugh harder than anyone has ever made you laugh, or who holds your hand in public and smiles at you in a way you haven't had somebody do for years, or who is really, really great with your dog—but somehow makes you feel constantly miserable and insecure. Please, the minute you realize the situation is making you feel depressed and hurt and it's really not going to go the way you want it to, please put an end to it as soon as you can. It's nice to have a break from being completely and utterly single, but only you will know when the price you're paying for that is too high. However, we—this book—will always be here to remind you of what a superfox you are. Please read it when you forget. You are far too precious to let any man make you feel like less than what you are—a magnificent woman worthy of great love.

frequently asked questions

Dear Greg and Liz,

What if I'm just not that into him? Did you ever think of that, huh? Why do you just assume it's only guys who aren't into girls? Why don't you write a book called *She's Just Not That Into You?*

Fiona

FROM THE DESK OF GREG

Hey Shouty,

Keep it down. If we wrote a book called *She's Just Not That Into You*, it would sell eight copies. Men don't process heartbreak that way. We don't run to Barnes & Noble and buy a book. We get drunk and stand on your lawn, then the cop comes and we're fairly sure it's over. But seriously, of course it goes both ways. How would I know what I know had I not been in the same position

180

you may find yourself in now—hopelessly pining over someone unwilling to give me affection? Yes, it applies to men—and as soon as they start reading, we'll start writing.

Dear Shouty,

I understand why you are asking that, though. You want us to acknowledge that sometimes, often, women reject men, that men are not these almighty beings that hold all the power. So let me be clear for both Greg and myself: We know that women go around breaking up with men, rejecting men, all the time. We don't believe that our readers are these pathetic creatures who get rejected on a regular basis. (I'm not a pathetic, undesirable creature who gets rejected on a regular basis! Those are just the particular stories I shared for the benefit of this book! Honest!) It just so happens that our book addresses the phenomenon of how *women* behave when men are rejecting them—which is uniquely feminine. I have so far in my lifetime never had a male friend replay a voice mail for me from a girl he's been dating because he wants to know if she "really, really likes" him. In short, this book is about the excuses women give for men who are just not that into them. Therefore we talk a lot about men who are not that into women. But we fully acknowledge that women break men's hearts all the time, and we are only representing a segment of all the nutty things going on out there in the dating world.

Dear Greg,

You never mention anything about single mothers in your book. It's so much harder for us. Do you know how impossible it is to meet a man who wants to date a woman with children? Maybe I *do* have to settle for someone who isn't that into me. In my situation, can't I really say it's better than nothing?

Parker

FROM THE DESK OF GREG

Dear Singled Out,

I'm not in your situation so I can't say if it's better than nothing, but let me acknowledge this. I do know how hard it is, as I work with women and have friends who are single moms. But my advice to them is always the same: You deserve to be in an awesome relationship with somebody who respects your needs—*especially* because you have kids. What little time you can give to that relationship, shouldn't it be great? I also tell single moms that it's all in the way you frame it. Remember, anyone who dates you has the distinct pleasure of being allowed into the inner sanctum of your family. You don't just let anyone in. Set the tone at the beginning and expect great things for yourself because you deserve them, Supermom.

Dear Greg,

Does this book apply to married couples? I mean, what if I suspect my husband is just not that into me? Isn't it different once you're married?

Hannah

FROM THE DESK OF GREG

Dear Wedding Belle,

Marriage, particularly when there are children, is harder to walk away from. Ask if the problems can be fixed, and if they cannot my answer's the same. We didn't come here to be in loveless relationships with people who don't respect us. This might be controversial, but I believe marriage is just a relationship tied to a legal document. It shouldn't be an excuse to be miserable for the rest of your life.

Also, I have many friends who grew up with parents who were just not that into each other, and a hundred percent of them wished their parents had left and found happiness so they could have some model for what that is.

Dear Greg,

I broke up with my girlfriend because she's a raving psycho. Sometimes guys are just not into girls because they're raving lunatics. Why don't you ever mention that sometimes it's their fault that we're just not that into them?

Bryan

FROM THE DESK OF GREG

Dear Man Show,

Buddy, if you want to write that book, go ahead. But I don't think you're going to sell too many copies of *It's All Your Fault, You Crazy Bitch*. As for us, we were working under the assumption that many women already blame themselves too much. This book is for the woman who sits there for days wondering what she did wrong when a guy doesn't call her back. Or the woman who tells herself that it's her fault that her husband cheated on her. Or the woman who hates herself because that guy at work won't ask her out. I want the women reading our book to know that they're not bad just because someone doesn't like them. So maybe a couple of women who read this book really are bad and remain clueless lunatics. I can live with that.

Dear Greg,
How do I give this book to a friend and not hurt her feelings?

Ilana

Dear Great Taste in Books,   FROM THE DESK OF GREG

What I have suggested is asking your friend if she is a fan of *Sex and the City*. Then you can give her the book and tell her it's from "two funny writers from *Sex and the City*." Of course, now that I've just written this in the book, I've blown your cover. In this case, just tell her you really care about her and that the book is really funny.

Dear Greg,
I hated your book.

Talia

Dear Who Needs a Hug,

Awesome. I always tell people, "If you hated our book, that's fine. At least you have an opinion." But if you liked our book, I say, "What's your name? Would you like some chocolate?" (See? It's better to like our book. Then you get chocolate.)

Dear Greg,

Oh my God! I finally got it! Your book makes so much sense to me now! After finally breaking up with that married guy, and then dating that *psychopath*, and then getting dumped by my boss and losing my job, I finally realized that everything you said in your book is true! I'm so sorry it took me so long to see the light!! And you know what's really cool now? When I even suspect a guy is just not that into me—like if he's ten minutes late, or if he makes a lame excuse like he can't see me because his sister's in the hospital—I just break up with him. Or at least totally freak out on him. One guy had to cancel a date because he sprained an ankle. So I just walked right into that emergency room and said to him flat out, "Listen, if you're just not that into me, just tell me." Thank you so much, Greg—you have really empowered me!!

Nikki

Dear Nikki,

Oh, Nikki, Nikki, Nikki. When we were writing the book, we were hoping for a reaction from our readers— not an overreaction. This book was meant to be used for good, not evil. It was meant to be our little secret—a handy little tool that helped you see what was really going on in your relationships. And when I say "tool," I don't mean a giant shovel you use to hit unsuspecting men over the head. I mean something you use, combined with your own good judgment and self-esteem, to make healthy decisions for yourself. I know this book might seem like the Bible to you right now, but it's actually been out for only two years and was published by Simon Spotlight Entertainment—not God. So please remember: The book may work in mysterious ways, but if you stay crazy, Nikki, it's never going to do you a damn bit of good.

Oh, never mind.

Dear Greg,

After all this time, haven't you come to your senses about your whole "girls can't ask out guys" thing?

Andrea

Dear Dead Horse,

I am loathe to advise anyone not to participate in their life, i.e., not asking out someone whom you find attractive. However, I still think you're worth being asked out.

To close, I have to say it has been a very humbling experience, writing this book, then entering into a prolonged discussion with single women about their love lives. I was particularly struck with how hard it is for women to date in this world. And even though I was empathetic before, I am even more so now, having met so many of you and having read your stories and heard your tales. There are days where I agree with Liz, who often feels that there are not enough good men to go around. Then I meet a woman who dumped the guy who caused her so much pain and is now happily with someone else, or I talk to a woman who is still out there looking but is loving her life, and I am reinspired right along with you.

Finally I will say this as loudly as I can: We think all people—men, women, gay, straight, or otherwise—are entitled to awesome relationships while they are enjoying their stay here on Earth. And we hope that this book was helpful, but if not, take what you need, leave the rest, and go find a way that works, so you too can have what you so richly deserve—love.

—Greg

ABOUT THE AUTHORS

Comedian **Greg Behrendt** was a consultant for three consecutive seasons on *Sex and the City* and is the coauthor of the *New York Times* bestseller *It's Called a Breakup Because It's Broken* and a forthcoming guide to the art of dating. Behrendt is the host of *The Greg Behrendt Show* as well as a prime-time reality show about relationships, *Greg Behrendt's Wake-Up Call*, set to debut in 2007. His acclaimed stand-up comedy has been seen on HBO, Comedy Central, *The Tonight Show*, *Late Show with David Letterman*, and *Late Night with Conan O'Brien*. He lives in Los Angeles with his wife and two daughters.

Liz Tuccillo was an executive story editor of HBO's Emmy-winning *Sex and the City* and is the author of the upcoming book *How to Be Single* for Simon & Schuster's Atria Books. She is currently living and dating in New York City.